ÖDÏNANÏ: THE IGBO I

**OKUKU ANAAGÖ MMADÜAGWU (ASHÏÏ).
Ö BALÜ DIKE EGWU.
OTIGBU ONYE NA-ETIGBU ONYE SÖ YA KWÜ.**

Author: Emmanuel Kaanaenechukwu ANIZOBA
(EZEANA, ABÖSHÏ-UDUGHUDU-NGAGWU-DÏ-IGBO-EGWU)

Order this book online at www.trafford.com/08-0487
or email orders@trafford.com

Most Trafford titles are also available at major online book retailers.

Note for Librarians: A cataloguing record for this book is available from Library
and Archives Canada at www.collectionscanada.ca/amicus/index-e.html

ISBN: 978-1-4251-7611-2

*We at Trafford believe that it is the responsibility of us all, as both individuals
and corporations, to make choices that are environmentally and socially sound.
You, in turn, are supporting this responsible conduct each time you purchase a
Trafford book, or make use of our publishing services. To find out how you are
helping, please visit www.trafford.com/responsiblepublishing.html*

*Our mission is to efficiently provide the world's finest, most comprehensive
book publishing service, enabling every author to experience success.
To find out how to publish your book, your way, and have it available
worldwide, visit us online at www.trafford.com/10510*

www.trafford.com

North America & international
toll-free: 1 888 232 4444 (USA & Canada)
phone: 250 383 6864 ♦ fax: 250 383 6804
email: info@trafford.com

The United Kingdom & Europe
phone: +44 (0)1865 487 395 ♦ local rate: 0845 230 9601
facsimile: +44 (0)1865 481 507 ♦ email: info.uk@trafford.com

10 9 8 7 6 5 4 3 2

DEDICATION

This book is dedicated to:

Chi Ukwu, Chukwu or Amaamaamachaamacha (the Great God, the Unknown Godhead), Chi na-eke, Chineke, Mmöö or Ndü (God the Creator, the Son and Word of the Godhead, Spirit, Life), Alüshï (the Gods and their Spirit Hosts), Ndï Otu (Spirit Guilds of the Elements: Earth, Water, Air and Fire), Chi m or Oke-Chukwu m (my personal God or my share of God and Life).

Ichie Ukwu na Ichie Nta, Ökpü Ukwu na Ökpü Nta (My male and female Parents, dead or alive); particularly my great grandfather Udoh Anaagö, high priest of the Earth-God Ana or Anï (whose shrine is Aja-Ana or Aja-Anï) of Agülü Öka (Agulu Awka), Nigeria; whose re-incarnation I am.

The entire Anïzöö Udoh family, holders of the Öfö na Alö (the symbols of power and authority) of the Anaagö Mmadüagwu lineage.

My village Ümübeele and my town Öka na-asö enwe (Awka, for which the monkey is sacred).

All lovers of Ödïnanï or Omenana, the Igbo religion.

CONTENTS

About the Author, Emmanuel K. Anizoba:

A BIOGRAPHICAL NOTE

Born in 1945, Emmanuel K. Anizoba was brought up in a Christian family with a strong Polytheistic ancestry, in Umubele village of the blacksmith town Awka, Anambra State, Nigeria. Son of a government teacher, he accompanied his father during the latter's movements from one school to another and attended government primary schools at Ajali, Awka and Afikpo. A very turbulent youth, he attended secondary school at Okongwu Memorial Grammar School Nnewi (1960-63) and Igwebuike Grammar School Awka (1964). Having performed poorly at the end of his secondary school career (bagged a grade 3 school leaving certificate!), he entered the civil service in 1965 at Enugu as a finance clerk from where he joined the Biafran army (July 1967—January 1970).

In June 1970, his eldest sister, Rose Anizoba, invited him to Geneva, Switzerland, to study French in order to gain admission to study economics at the University of Fribourg. At Fribourg, he got a Licence ès Sciences Economiques et Sociales in 1976 and in 1979 he got a PhD in Econometrics. He was on the Dean's list at the University of Fribourg and was appointed Teaching Assistant to the Econometrics Chair. In 1980 he left Switzerland for Nigeria, where he continued his brief teaching career at the University of Port Harcourt.

He joined the African Development Bank (AfDB) in 1981 as a Statistician Economist. At the AfDB he managed the Loan Accounting & Financial Statistics Division (1996—2001) before being appointed Advisor to AfDB's Financial Controller in 2002.

At the age of sixty years, Emmanuel K. Anizoba retired from the AfDB in April 2005. He settled in his Umubele village Awka home, where efforts are underway to revive the polytheistic and living tradition of his ancestors. He is married and has five children.

1
PREAMBLE

BASIC PHILOSOPHY

In an attempt to explain the origin of the manifest universe, the first verse of the Christian Bible says:

"In the beginning God created the heaven and the earth." (Gen 1:1)

But we may rightly ask:

(1) In what place did the action of creating take place?
(2) Had the manifest universe any beginning?
(3) Where did this creative God come from?
(4) Where did this God get the materials or stuff with which to create the heaven and the earth?

These four questions constitute a philosophical nightmare for the untutored Christian. No logical explanation of the origin of the manifest universe is possible without logical answers to these questions. We shall provide answers to the questions in accordance with Ancient Wisdom.

(1) In what place did the action of creating taking place? In Space! To choose any other locus leads to a blind alley and insuperable problems of logic.

(2) Had the manifest universe any beginning? No! The universe

emerges from Space, stays in Space for some time, and dissolves back into Space—ad infinitum. Just in the same manner that ice emerges from a body of water, floats in the water for some time, and dissolves back into the water. It is the serpent swallowing its tail, a circle with neither beginning nor end. Recall the Christian chant: Etu ö dï na mbüü, öö dï ügbüaa, ö ga-adïgïdee ootuaa, wee luo n'üwa ebighiebi, Amen! As it was in the beginning, it is now, and ever shall be, world without end, Amen!

(3)   Where did this creative God come from? It is there in Space! Does the bolt of lightning or the tornado come from somewhere other than Space? No! Their home is Space. Space may be empty of objects, but It is not empty. The term "empty space" has no meaning.

(4)   Where did this God get the materials or stuff with which to create the heaven and the earth? From Space of course! Space contains all that is required for the construction of the manifest universe. To create, the God needs some world-stuff because ex nihilo, nihil fit, nothing comes from nothing. Creation by sheer fiat is nonsense.

So, Space is the absolute Container of all that is, whether manifested or unmanifested. And Space is that which was, is and will be, whether there is a Universe or not; whether there be Gods or none.

Since Space is the all, we may ask: What is Space?

Nobody knows! It is the undefined and indefinable term in the logic that tries to explain the origin of the manifest universe. It is the same with a term like electricity: what is electricity? Nobody knows! It's an undefined and indefinable term in physics. To call it energy does not define it! And what is energy? This is an infinite regressus or a circle. We must assume such terms as given, as the basis for ulterior constructions and reasoning. We are mentally stuck without assuming them as given.

Hence, the basic assumption of the Ancients is: Infinite Space is the Absolute Deity, which has neither name nor attribute. It is the Unknown Deity or Godhead. And the differentiation or crystallization of Infinite Space is symbolized in the Hierarchy of Beings that people the cosmogony of all nations.

Space as the Unknown Deity appears clearly in the Christian Bible where St. Paul says the following in the book of Acts 17:23-28 concerning the Unknown God:

23. For as I was passing through and considering the objects of your

worship, I even found an altar with this inscription: TO THE UNKNOWN GOD. Therefore, the One whom you worship without knowing, Him I proclaim to you:

24. God, who made the world and everything in it, since He is Lord of heaven and earth, does not dwell in temples made with hands.

25. Nor is He worshiped with men's hands, as though He needed anything, since He gives to all life, breath, and all things.

26. And He has made from one blood every nation of men to dwell on all the face of the earth, and has determined their pre-appointed times and the boundaries of their dwellings,

27. So that they should seek the Lord, in the hope that they might grope for Him and find Him, though He is not far from each one of us;

28. For in Him we live and move and have our being, as also some of your own poets have said, For we are also His offspring."

In verse 28 above St Paul tells us, "For in Him [the Unknown God] we live, and move, and have our being.

Question: In what do we live, and move, and have our being?

Answer: In Space of course!

The Ancients tell us that this Space in which we live is a delimited portion of Infinite Space. They call the Space we live in Bright Space. And Infinite Space they call Dark Space or Darkness.

Infinite Space is living Being and periodically gives birth to the Bright Space of manifestation and existence. Since all that is born must die, the Bright Space is re-absorbed into Infinite Space in due season.

We are told that Infinite Space is a fused triune Reality comprising consciousness, the content of consciousness and the power that relates consciousness to its content. Periodically, this relating power chooses a portion of Infinite Space for a separation of the fused consciousness and its content into subjects related to objects. This separation results in the birth of a system of reflective awareness, a Mind. A discrimination is made between Self and Not-Self, Light and Darkness, subjectivity and objectivity. Thus Bright Space or Universal Mind is born from the Darkness of Infinite Space. And Bright Space is like a gigantic sphere floating in Dark Space; a mighty jellyfish floating in a boundless ocean.

With this birth, a Ring of Power now delimits the extent of the Bright Space of manifestation within the all-containing parent of Infinite Space. In due season, the Ring of Power collapses and existence is resolved back into non-existence. And Bright Space melts back into its parent Infinite Space.

Next, the Power that brought about the primal subject-object separation within Infinite Space fills that Bright Space or Universal Mind with four categories of simple triune existents or individual Minds, called Monads. A Monad is an entity made up of the three primal principles of being, which under a specific set of circumstances will produce a specific form and/or sequence of events. Thus a Monad here means the first possible and most simple existent, and no entity can exist that does not partake of the three primal principles of being, i.e., consciousness, the content of consciousness, and the power that relates consciousness to its content.

These four groups of Monads or fragments of the Universal Mind are distinguished by their modes of operation which appear as mineral, plant, animal and human types of conscious activity. In other words, the oceans, the Earth, everything we see manifesting as mineral, plant, animal and human forms are all crystallized Space. And this crystallization is achieved by the same Power that effected the initial subject-object separation.

The Universal Mind is thus presented as being composed of a four-fold hierarchy of triune Monads, destined to manifest the various patterns inherent in the Power that brought them into existence. This Power, we are told, is Life. That this Life is the creative living God is easily seen by replacing "the Word" with "Life" in the following verses of St John's gospel in the (KJV) Bible: John 1:1- 4, 9

1. In the beginning was Life [the Word], and Life [the Word] was with God, and Life [the Word] was God.

2. The same [Life] was in the beginning with God.

3. All things were made by Life [him]; and without Life [him] was not any thing made that was made.

4. In him [Life] was [particularized] life; and the [particularized] life was the light of men.

9. That [Life] was the true Light, which lighteth every man that cometh into the world.

No cosmogony, the world over, with the sole exception of the Christian, has ever attributed to the One Highest cause, the Universal Deific Principle, the immediate creation of our Earth, man, or anything connected with these. This statement holds as good for the Hebrew or Chaldean Kabala as it does for Genesis, had the latter been ever thoroughly understood, and—what is still more important—correctly translated. The same reserve is found in the Talmud and in every national system of religion whether monotheistic or exoterically polytheistic. From the superb religious poem by the Kabalist Rabbi Solomon Ben Gabirol in "the Kether Malchuth," we select a few definitions given in the prayers of Kippur:

"Thou art one, the beginning of all numbers, and the foundation of all edifices; Thou art one, and in the secret of Thy unity the wisest of men are lost, because they know it not. Thou art one, and Thy Unity is never diminished, never extended, and cannot be changed. Thou art one, but not as an element of numeration; for Thy Unity admits not of multiplication, change or form. Thou art Existent; but the understanding and vision of mortals cannot attain to thy existence, nor determine for thee the Where, the How, and the Why. Thou art Existent, but in thyself alone, there being none other that can exist with thee. Thou art Existent, before all time and without Place. Thou art Existent, and thy existence is so profound and secret that none can penetrate and discover thy secrecy. Thou art Living, but within no time that can be fixed or known; Thou art Living, but not by a spirit or a soul, for Thou art thyself, The Soul of All Souls." etc., etc.

There is a distance between this Kabalistic Deity and the Biblical Jehovah, the spiteful and revengeful God of Abram, Isaac, and Jacob, who tempted the former and wrestled with the last. No true philosopher but would repudiate such a Deity.

Everywhere there is either a Logos (Word)—a "Light shining in Darkness," truly—or the Architect of the Worlds is esoterically a plural number. The Latin Church, paradoxical as ever, while applying the epithet of Creator to Jehovah alone, adopts a plethora of names for the working Forces of the latter, those names betraying the secret. For if the said Forces had nothing to do with "Creation" so-called, why call them Elohim (Alhim) in plural; "divine workmen" and Energies (Energeia), incandescent celestial stones (lapides igniti coelorum), and especially, "supporters of the World" (Kosmokratores), governors or Rulers of the World (rectores mundi), the "Wheels" of the World (Rotae), Ophanim, Flames and Powers, "Sons of God" (B'ne Alhim, Benai Elohim), "Vigilant Counsellors," etc., etc.

Primary Creation is called the Creation of Light (Spirit); and the Secondary—that of Darkness (world-stuff, matter). Both are found in Genesis 1:2 and Genesis 2:1, viz.:

(1)   Gen 1:2 "And the earth was without form, and void; and darkness was upon the face of the deep. And the Spirit of God

moved upon the face of the waters."

(2) Gen 2:1 "Thus the heavens and the earth were finished, and all the host of them."

The first is the emanation of self-born Gods (Elohim); the second of physical nature.

This is why it is said in the Zohar: "Oh, companions, companions, man as emanation was both man and woman; as well on the side of the Father as on the side of the Mother. And this is the sense of the words: And Elohim spoke: 'Let there be Light and it was Light!' . . . And this is the 'two-fold man'"

"Man and woman on the side of the Father" (Spirit) refers to Primary Creation; and on the side of the Mother (mind-stuff or matter) to the Secondary. The two-fold man is Adam Kadmon, the male and female abstract prototype (the Divine Plan) and the differentiated Elohim (the Gods). Man is a "Fallen Angel," a god in exile.

The human mind is that sacred spark of the Universal Mind which burns and expands into the flower of human reason and self-consciousness. It is this human mind that we find in Genesis 2:9 referred to as the Tree of Knowledge of Good and Evil, whose fruit Adam and Eve were forbidden to eat. Thanks to Satan, the couple ate the forbidden fruit and became as the Gods (Elohim), knowing good and evil. We read in Genesis 3:22: "And the LORD God said, Behold, the man is become as one of us, to know good and evil: and now, lest he put forth his hand, and take also of the tree of life, and eat, and live for ever." Man rises to the hierarchy of Gods when his spirit and mind are welded together in the aeonial incarnational task of wedding the mortal mind with the immortal spirit.

In spite of all efforts to the contrary, Christian theology—having burdened itself with the Hebrew esoteric account of the creation of man, which is understood literally—cannot find any reasonable excuse for its "God, the Creator," who produces a man devoid of mind and sense; nor can it justify the punishment following an act, for which Adam and Eve might plead non compos mentis (mentally incompetent). For if the couple is admitted to be ignorant of good and evil before the eating of the forbidden fruit, how could it be expected to know that disobedience was evil? If primeval man was meant to remain a half-witted, or rather witless, being, then his creation was aimless and even cruel, if produced by an omnipotent and perfect God. But Adam and Eve are shown, even in Genesis, to be created by a class of lower divine Beings, the Elohim, who are so jealous of their personal prerogatives as reasonable and intelligent creatures, that they will not allow man to become "as one of us." This is plain, even from the dead-letter meaning of the Bible. The Gnostics, then, were right in regarding the Jewish God as belonging to a class of lower, material and not very holy denizens of the invisible World.

The Beings, or the Being, collectively called Elohim, who first (if ever) pronounced the cruel words, "Behold, the man is become as one of us, to know good and evil; and now, lest he put forth his hand and take also of the tree of life and eat and live for ever ..." must have been indeed the Ilda-baoth, the Demiurge of the Nazarenes, filled with rage and envy against his own creature, whose reflection created Ophiomorphos. In this case it is but natural—even from the dead letter standpoint—to view Satan, the Serpent of Genesis, as the real creator and benefactor, the Father of Spiritual mankind. For it is he who was the "Harbinger of Light," bright radiant Lucifer, who opened the eyes of the automaton created, as alleged, by Jehovah. And he who was the first to whisper, "in the day ye eat thereof ye shall be as Elohim, knowing good and evil," can only be regarded as a Saviour. An "adversary" to Jehovah the "personating spirit," he still remains in esoteric truth the ever-loving "Messenger" (the angel), the Seraphim and Cherubim who both knew well and loved still more, and who conferred on us spiritual, instead of physical immortality—the latter a kind of static immortality that would have transformed man into an undying "Wandering Jew."

Man, being a compound of the essences of all the celestial Hierarchies may succeed in making himself, as such, superior, in one sense, to any hierarchy or class, or even combination of them. "Man can neither propitiate nor command the Gods," it is said. But, by transcending his senses, and arriving thereby at the full knowledge of the non-separateness of his spirit from the One universal Spirit, man can, even during his terrestrial life, become as "One of Us." Thus it is, by eating of the fruit of knowledge (using his mind) which dispels ignorance that man becomes like one of the Elohim or the Archangels (Ruling Gods); and once on their plane the spirit of solidarity and perfect harmony, which reigns in every hierarchy, must extend over him and protect him in every particular.

CLARIFICATION OF TERMS

Our objective is to explain Ödïnanï, the Igbo religion. Since the subject uses terms such as religion, God, Gods, Spirit, Spirits, universe, man, etc., it will be helpful to state what we understand by these terms. It is dishonest for me to ask someone whether he believes in "God" without first telling him what the word "God" stands for. To assume that he should know, since it is "common knowledge", is bigotry on my part. The fellow will put me in a tight corner if he has the intelligence to ask me for a definition of my "God", in order to help him decide whether he believes or not in the thing defined.

Religion is the science that relates man to God and the universe around him. As a science, it is a systematically organized body of knowledge about man, the universe and God. Religion teaches us that God is either manifest or unmanifest. The unmanifest God is the Godhead or Infinite Space, from which the manifest and creative God emerges to give itself a body that we call the universe. The unmanifest Godhead is the Infinite Space in which we live and move and have our being. The manifest God is Cosmic or Universal Spirit, manifesting in all and through all as a ceaseless unerring intelligence. The universe is the body of this manifest God.

And what is Spirit? Spirit is Breath or Wind, as we may easily verify by consulting Strong's Hebrew and Greek Dictionaries. In Hebrew Spirit is given by Neshamah or Ruach and both denote Breath or Wind. In Greek equally, Spirit is given by Pneuma denoting Breath or Wind again.

The unmanifest Godhead is the Infinite Space in which we live and move and have our being. It is the Unknown God of the Bible described in the book of Acts 17:23-28. Religion is able to make statements about the unmanifest Godhead through deductions that derive from the study of the manifest creative God.

Since Spirit means Breath or Wind, we may agree that:
1. Its domain is the whole of Space
2. Its acts are seen and felt, but It is invisible;
3. It is neither female nor male;
4. It moves without feet and grasps without a hand.

The manifest God or Spirit is the great river that links the universe to its source in the unmanifest God or Godhead. The Godhead is the source of all that is manifest. The Spirit or manifest God is the agency through which manifestation is effected. The manifest God is the only Son of the Godhead. All things were made by this manifest God; and without It was not any thing made that was made. It is the Word of St. John's Gospel (John 1:1-4, 9).

Some of my readers accuse me of borrowing heavily from Christianity and of providing little or no documented local evidence to back my assertions concerning Ödïnanï. I reply that research has shown that Christianity is Ödïnanï—disfigured and varnished. This is the modus operandi of Christianity: the torching of the library of Alexandria, the razing of Pagan temples, etc., were all intended to mask the origins of the doctrines presented by ascendant Christianity as divine revelation. Having discovered what Christianity did to Ödïnanï and how it happened, polemics on the issue would be futile. By carefully removing the varnish and interpolations that Christianity has used to mask its parenthood, I am able to recuperate the beautiful, rational and robust cult of my Igbo ancestors—Ödïnanï.

The Godhead is the container and Source of all. God or Spirit is the Power that unfolds the inaccessible contents of the Godhead into what we call a manifested universe of creatures. Religion is the science that teaches man about himself, about the universe of which he is a part, and about the manifest God which links everything to its source in the Godhead. Recall that religion comes from re ligio, which means to tie back to a source or to yoke. Worship of God describes the ways we choose to commune with the manifest God and, through It, with the Godhead—the Source. Men worship God in diverse, but equivalent, ways. The God is the same—Spirit, Mmöö—but the rituals or methods for approaching It differ. We may now understand the stupidity of the dichotomy: ndï üka (Christians) and ndï ö-gö mmöö (spirit worshipers). Whatever the religion, we are all ndï ö-gö mmöö or spirit worshipers.

What we call religions are actually different, but equivalent, methods of expressing the same science—Religion. It is thus improper and misleading to talk about religions: Christian religion, Moslem religion, Hindu religion, and what not. These are cults at best, but not religions. Religion is a science, not sciences.

Continuing our clarification process the following is a brief description of the levels of Being from the Godhead to the universe of forms. We provide here the basics for the understanding of Pagan philosophy, which is at the foundation of Christian religious thought.

THE GODHEAD

This is the unmanifest origin of all things. It is Non-Existence, because ex-ist-ence signifies a standing forth. This is the level of Being in

ÖDĪNANĪ: THE IGBO RELIGION

latency, which is named Chaos, Darkness, Unknown God, or Infinite Space. It is the fused state of the triune aspect of Being comprising: Consciousness, the Content of Consciousness and Power (the Spirit or Will) that relates Consciousness to its Content. Manifestation or creation is the cyclical unfoldment of the fused Godhead, resulting in a living universe. Dissolution follows unfoldment, ad infinitum. Just as day follows night, it is worlds without end or the serpent swallowing its tail. Between manifestations all is withdrawn into the Darkness of Non-Existence. The Spirit is the power that holds together the two poles of the Godhead and, in due season, the same Spirit unfolds the fused contents of the Godhead to produce a living universe. It is this unfoldment that we call creation. This Spirit is the Breath, Will or Word (Logos) of the Godhead. It is the outgoing Son of the hidden Father-Mother, the One Life, the Intelligent Electric Entity.

MANIFESTATION: FROM THE INVISIBLE TO THE VISIBLE

St. Paul says: "That which may be known of God is manifest; for the invisible things of him from the creation of the world are clearly seen, being understood from those things which are made, even his eternal power and Godhood." (Rom 1:20)

Thus, man needs only to look at the world of outer things and their phenomena to see a perfect replica of all higher things, the realities of the super-world of spiritual being. If he longs for truth, he has only to open his eyes on the world outside him to behold the forms and norms of truth materialized in living concreteness before him.

To be sure, he must be taught to pierce through the opacity of the form before him to discover the structure of truth that is there in living reality. This art can be acquired, although it is an art demanding the highest philosophical astuteness. It requires not so much the exertion of brilliant genius as the intellectual sincerity of naïve directness. It takes not the sophistication of intellect but the straightforward candor of the mind in registering what one sees. It is an opening of the eye to clear seeing. It must be urged to discovery by the antecedent knowledge that nature is such an open book, whose pages, paragraphs and sentences are the phenomena in every field, wood, lake, brook, garden, hill and glade. For the true doctrine of the Omnipresence is that God is present in all Its parts in every moss and cobweb.

The significance of this principle is found in the Hebrew Talmud, where we read: "If thou wilt know the invisible, open wide thine eyes on the visible."

If man will not open wide his eyes on the visible he will have no basic model or pattern by which to sharpen his apprehension of truth. Through his immersion in the actual world he has the opportunity to acquaint his mind with the divinely certified forms of truth. He can never generate a faculty for the recognition of truth unless he lets life train his mind in her school of contact with the living forms of that truth which she presents in profusion. This instruction is part of the purpose for which spirits and souls are sent out among the planets. How would life teach her children if she did not furnish them with models of the things they are to learn? In short, how can one study unless one looks at what is to be studied?

Man's only sure road to apprehension of the sublime things of the invisible worlds, the laws, principles and structure of the cosmos, is to travel the highway of the visible world he is a native of. All pursuit of knowledge at a high level can result in gain for him only through his power to interpret data on the basis of his own experience with reality. Higher things can have meaning for him only on the grounds of their reference to what he knows through his living contact with the actual. If higher truth takes him into a world of things intellectually exotic, bizarre and unrelated to his normal frame of recognitions, such truth will only bewilder him. Supernal truth must come to have relevance for him in the light of what has made sense and meaning to him in his experience with palpable things. If it totally transcends his known world, it will have no message for him. Truth is but one system, and its forms of manifestation in any world, kingdom or plane of life are microcosmic or macrocosmic reduplications of its form in the world of archetypes. The phenomena of physical life in our world make a graphic panorama of all the fundamental archai or principles of being. The Greeks said that if man would come to know himself, he would by that know all the secrets, laws and meanings of the universe. For man himself is a miniature eidolon of the macrocosm, as a seed is the entire structure of its parent tree or plant in potentiality.

We may liken the idea of manifestation to that of a builder who desires to build a great Palace, viz.:

1. He grasps in his mind the plan of the whole building. The manifest God proceeds likewise by setting out the Divine Plan, which is the Absolute form of all that exists. This is the source of all forms, the Deific Form, the Celestial or Archetypal Man, the Adam Kadmon of the Hebrews.

2.   Our builder then considers the way according to which the work shall be done, that it shall correspond to the plan. He maps out the building team in accordance with the plan. Similarly, the manifest God or Spirit shares out Itself, creating a hierarchy of Spirits who will build the Universe according to the Divine Plan and then inhabit it. These Spirits are pure Breaths or Essences, the Immortal natures.

3.   Then the builder considers the material needed for the construction. The steel rods, binding wire, sand, stones, bricks, mortar, planks, etc., must be assembled. In the same manner, the Spirit needs some stuff to construct the visible Universe. It needs some world-stuff because ex nihilo, nihil fit, nothing comes from nothing. Creation by sheer fiat is nonsense. While reading the Bible in school I found in Genesis: "And God said, Let there be light: and there was light." (Gen 1:3) Neither my Sunday school priest-teacher in primary school nor my Bible Knowledge teacher in secondary school was able to tell me where God got the light from. I was, instead, reprimanded for my impertinence in questioning the content of the Bible and the omnipotence of God. In retrospect I feel sorry for these teachers who, because the Bible says so, propagated lies about a God they knew nothing about. The omnipotent first creates the world-stuff, ensouls it with a part of itself and sets it into a vibratory motion that produces light. Continuing our builder analogy, the Spirit creates the abode of Minds, i.e., triune entities (consciousness, spirit and content of consciousness). This is the needed world-stuff or material for the construction of forms, the mortal natures.

4.   Finally, the builder effects the actual construction with the relevant workers and building materials, in accordance with the plan. Similarly, the Spirit creates the abode of spirits united with minds and form, all in accordance with the archetypal models.

Let's explain further the ideas contained in the four points above.

Within the Godhead of Infinite Space, the Spirit delimits a portion whose content will furnish the basis of future differentiations. This portion of space earmarked for manifestation is thus bounded by a spirit-ring or firmament. The waters of space are thus divided into those above this firmament (outside the bounded space) and those below the firmament (within the bounded space). The Spirit lays out the prototype of the forthcoming manifestation—the model of things to come. And then shares itself out into hierarchies of effectuating powers who will, using the enclosed triune content of the Godhead, produce and run a universe in accordance with the given prototype. This is the creation of the Gods. This sharing out of the Spirit provides us with the various essences which build, animate and rule the universe from within. It is the Universal Spirit, the Sons of God (Fiery Sparks) who build forms and ensoul those forms as incarnating spirits. They are the Prodigal Sons and Eternal Pilgrims, who go out into the worlds to suffer and cause suffering.

The divine worker has chosen a portion of space for the manifestation of the Godhead. He has laid out the plan of the universe, a plan brought from the Darkness. He has shared out himself in accordance with the work ahead. Since the mortar is already available (the Spirit itself), we need living bricks to move forward with the construction of a living universe.

The living bricks come from the first differentiation of the enclosed portion of the Chaos resulting in the birth of Universal Mind—a system of related awareness. Thus, in the circumscribed portion of Infinite Space the Spirit brings to birth the Universal Mind, also called the Great Monad or Great Soul of the universe. A portion of the fused Chaos is now set apart or differentiated into a relation, or Mind, made up of: Consciousness, the Relating Power (Spirit), and the Content of Consciousness.

Consciousness is the Knower or Subject pole of the knowing process, the Relating Power (Spirit) is the process of Knowing, and the Content of Consciousness is the Known or the Object pole of the knowing process.

The Spirit then divides Universal Mind into component minds and groups the latter into four functional levels, i.e., the One Mind (Great Monad, or Soul) becomes Many Minds (Monads, Souls). This is the creation of the world-stuff and these minds are the ultimate "bricks" of the universe, conscious bricks which will be built into the numerous grades of being that go to make up the manifest worlds. The Builders will move them into position in accord with the archetypal model. These monads are the basis of matter, the only matter in the universe, yet a matter that will be composed of empatterned organizations of energy around these individualized points in or of consciousness. The levels of the Universal Mind are, from the lowest to the highest:

(1) Physical level: For minds on this level the three aspects of Mind are proportional.

(2) Desire level: For minds on this level the power aspect dominates the other two.

(3) Lower mental level: For minds on this level the content aspect dominates the other two.

(4) Higher mental level: For minds on this level, the consciousness aspect of Mind is greater than the power and content aspects. Minds from this level are incorporated into form as individuals. The mind of man—the thinker—comes from this level of the Universal Mind.

Note that the Spirit is the first manifestation from the Godhead. It is called the Logos or Word of the Father/Mother hidden in the darkness of the Godhead. It is the manifest and knowable God, as against its unknown and unknowable status in the darkness of the Godhead. This is the Word spoken of in the first chapter of St. John's gospel. The identity of Spirit and Word is seen by replacing "Word" with "Spirit" in the relevant verses of St John's gospel in the (KJV) Bible: John 1:1-4, 9

1. In the beginning was the Word, and the Word was with God, and the Word was God.

2. The same was in the beginning with God.

3. All things were made by him; and without him was not any thing made that was made.

4. In him was life; and the life was the light of men.

9. That was the true Light, which lighteth every man that cometh into the world.

The beginning refers to the pre-manifestation fused state of the Godhead. The Spirit is the first to emerge from the Godhead, delimiting a portion of it with a view to unfolding its contents into a living universe. All things were truly made by him; and without him was not any thing made that was made. The Spirit creates the Universal Mind, differentiates it into component minds, builds forms with the differentiated elements and ensouls the forms with its Sparks; it is thus the true Light, which lighteth every man (and thing) that cometh into the world. It is Life.

The first-born of the Darkness, the Spirits, are the Life, the heart and pulse of the universe. The second are its Mind and the third are its Body.

FORMATION

Using monads from the four levels of the Universal Mind as building blocks, the universe of forms is built and inhabited by the hierarchies of the Spirit. We may note that the builder-spirits create forms in accordance with the prototypes in the archetypal world described above. The prototype is perfect, but the builders reproducing it are many and diversely talented. As a result, some copies of the original may be defective. Each form is the tabernacle of a spirit to which is attached a self-reflective apparatus or mind. The spirit, being breath, is given a body for action and a mind to embrace the universe in which it dwells. Every form in the universe has a resident spirit, a mind and a body. The universe is made up of solar systems, subject to universal law of hierarchical government. In our solar system our sun is a form endowed with a spirit and mind; the same is true of the planets of our system. The spirits of these planets are subservient to the spirit of the sun.

The elements (Earth, Water, Air and Fire) are made from the world-stuff above and inhabited by appropriate sparks from the spirit hierarchies.

On our planet Earth the forms are, from the lowest to the highest: Minerals, Plants, Animals, and Hominids.

From the above, we note that:

(1) Consciousness, the content of consciousness and the power that relates them (the spirit) are the three aspects of the Godhead, the Great Monad, and the Monads.

(2) Within the Godhead, the formed universe floats in the Universal Mind which, in turn, floats in the Universal Spirit.

(3) Forms are built and dissolved within the Universal Mind. At the close of the cycle of universal manifestation, the Spirit first withdraws itself from the universe; and the minds composing the latter return to their levels in the Universal Mind and resolve back into an undifferentiated mass. Finally, the firmament or Spirit-Ring around the Universal Mind collapses; and the waters above and below the firmament become one again. Cosmos returns to Chaos, its source. Existence returns to non-existence. Deity goes to sleep for a period equal in duration to the period of manifestation.

(4) The Universal Mind is the Father of the multitude of minds that make up its four levels. The four grades of Mind are the children of the same Father. But the minds of the higher mental level are called "Sons", because they are used as individual units in the construction of forms. They are "men" when com-

pared to the minds at the three lower levels of Mind. The mind of man—the thinker—comes from this level of the Universal Mind. When this mind merges itself with its associated incarnating spirit (the Christos), then an anointment and at-one-ment takes place and Christ is born in us. Thus the divine spirit, by this marriage with its associated mind, converts the latter to its own nature. This conversion is the object of the incarnation of spirit in forms. In his Timaeus Plato gives us the remarkable speech of the Demiurgus (Creative God) to the "junior Gods," who were the divine beings commissioned to come to earth and be the Gods embodied in an animal race that had no chance of reaching the next level of evolution without such tutelage. In it the Demiurgus enjoins the deities to come to earth and "unite mortal with immortal natures," promising them that they would "never be dissolved." The Ancients symbolized this at-one-ment of the personal spirit and mind by the winged globe: a solar disc (the spirit) with two wings (the bipolar mind). The senior Gods are those who have achieved this at-one-ment through hardwork and repeated incarnation. The following Bible extracts from the Book of Revelation refer to this at-one-ment and its associated rewards:

(1) Rev 2:7 He that hath an ear, let him hear what the Spirit saith unto the churches; To him that overcometh will I give to eat of the tree of life, which is in the midst of the paradise of God.

(2) Rev 2:11 He that hath an ear, let him hear what the Spirit saith unto the churches; He that overcometh shall not be hurt of the second death.

(3) Rev 2:17 He that hath an ear, let him hear what the Spirit saith unto the churches; To him that overcometh will I give to eat of the hidden manna, and will give him a white stone, and in the stone a new name written, which no man knoweth saving he that receiveth it.

(4) Rev 2:26 And he that overcometh, and keepeth my works unto the end, to him will I give power over the nations:

(5) Rev 3:5 He that overcometh, the same shall be clothed in white raiment; and I will not blot out his name out of the book of life, but I will confess his name before my Father, and before his angels.

(6) Rev 3:12 Him that overcometh will I make a pillar in the temple of my God, and he shall go no more out: and I will write upon

him the name of my God, and the name of the city of my God, which is new Jerusalem, which cometh down out of heaven from my God: and I will write upon him my new name.

(7) Rev 3:21 To him that overcometh will I grant to sit with me in my throne, even as I also overcame, and am set down with my Father in his throne.

(8) Rev 21:7 He that overcometh shall inherit all things; and I will be his God, and he shall be my son.

The statements "To him that overcometh," "Him that overcometh," and "He that overcometh" all refer to this aeonial task undertaken by the spirit to weld a mind to itself and become self-conscious. The incarnation of the Gods was really a sacrifice on their part. But sacrifice (Latin: sacra and facio) means "to make sacred", and has no immediate correlation with the denial to oneself of benefits. If privation came in the process of incarnation, it was incidental, not inherent. The spirit legions descended to make a lower order of life holy or sacred. Their labor was to sanctify with the gift of divinity the mortal race, and make it immortal and divine. But why is this at-one-ment so important for the incarnating spirit? Well, because the mind is the spirit's drawing room or workshop and sole instrument of reflective awareness. Since creation is always in the image and likeness of some model, the spirit uses its mind to create the requisite models. Concrete forms result from the accretion of the world-stuff around these models. See the author's book "The Second Birth. The Mind is a Bag. How Loaded is Yours?" It contains a complete description of this wedding of the spirit and mind.

(5) Manifestation may be described as creations as follows: (1) Creation of the archetypal form of the universe; the plan. (2) Creation of the Gods. It is they who build, inhabit and run the universe. (3) Creation of Mind and its partition into minds or world-stuff. (4) Creation of worlds or solar systems that compose the physical universe.

(6) The creations on Earth are those of Minerals, Plants, Animals, and Hominids including Man.

OUR SOLAR SYSTEM

Each form is the tabernacle of a spirit to which is attached a self-reflective apparatus or mind. The spirit, being breath, is given a body for action and a mind to embrace the universe in which it dwells. Thus, every form in the universe has a resident spirit and a mind. The universe is made up of solar systems, subject to universal law of hierarchical government.

In our solar system we find our Sun at its center, with planets and their moons orbiting this central Sun. As noted above our sun is a form endowed with a spirit and mind; the same is true of the planets and moons of our system. Our solar system is a micro-cosmos relative to the macro-cosmos of the great universe. And our micro-cosmos is an exact image or analogue, a miniature eidolon of the macro-cosmos. Both worlds are constituted in the same manner, function according to the same laws, and mutually influence each other through their corresponding parts.

The universe is bounded by a spirit-ring-pass-not. So is our solar system bounded by a spirit-ring that controls exchanges between our solar system and other solar systems. The universe has its grand archetypal world. So does our solar system have its archetypal world, which accords perfectly with the grand design. Like the universe, our solar system has its spirit hierarchies and the world-stuff for the building of forms. The entire universe being subject to hierarchical law, the same holds true for our solar cosmos. The spirits of the planets in the system are subservient to the spirit of the sun, their Lord.

Our planet Earth, like all forms, has a spirit endowed with a mind and a body. The spirits of everything living on Earth are subservient to its spirit. The spirit of man is subservient to the spirit of the Earth and the spirit of the latter is subservient to the spirit of the Sun. After the God in man (his spirit), the next God available to him is the God of the Earth. It is through the God of the Earth that man may have access to the God of the Sun and the Gods of other planets in our system. It is the neglect of this hierarchy of subservience that brought about the failure of solar religions or cults. Render to Caesar the things that are Caesar's, says Jesus. Only the cult or religion of the Earth God has the slightest chance of making any headway on the planet.

As indicated above, the elements (Earth, Water, Air and Fire) are made from the world-stuff above and inhabited by appropriate sparks from the spirit hierarchies.

On our planet Earth the forms are, from the lowest to the highest: Minerals, Plants, Animals, and Hominids (including man).

THE BASIS OF MORALS

Thus the component parts of man are: Body (Soma); Mind or Soul

(Psyche); Air, Wind or Spirit (Pneuma). The first element in man is the spirit or divine breath, which is equivalent to the pneuma of the Greeks (from pneo, "to breathe"), the Latin spiritus (from spiro, "to breathe"), and the Sanskrit atman (from an, "to blow, to breathe"). Spirit is the first "breath" from the Godhead. The second element is the mind. It is comparable to the Greek nous, the Latin mens, and Sanskrit manas. It is ruled by and forms the throne or vehicle of the spirit. The third element is the physical body, which corresponds to the Sanskrit sthula-sarira, the Latin corpus, and the Greek soma.

In every living form resides a manifesting spirit. All forms—whether stars, men, beasts, or the stones underneath our feet—are tabernacles for spirits, vital breaths, portions of the same Universal Breath or Spirit. And man sees truth when he realizes that he is one-in-spirit with all that is. This realization is the basis of ethics or morality.

In Matthew 22:34-40 we find Jesus giving the true basis of morals to the Pharisee lawyer:

34 But when the Pharisees had heard that he had put the Sadducees to silence, they were gathered together.

35 Then one of them, which was a lawyer, asked him a question, tempting him, and saying,

36 Master, which is the great commandment in the law?

37 Jesus said unto him, Thou shalt love the Lord thy God with all thy heart, and with all thy soul, and with all thy mind.

38 This is the first and great commandment.

39 And the second is like unto it, Thou shalt love thy neighbour as thyself.

40 On these two commandments hang all the law and the prophets.

Note that verse 37 above talks about "the Lord thy God" (the personal spirit) and not "the Lord God" (the Universal Spirit). Concerning the personal spirit, the Bible (KJV) says: "Know ye not that ye are the temple of God, and that the Spirit of God dwelleth in you?" (1Cor. 3:16) "What? know ye not that your body is the temple of the Holy Ghost which is in you, which ye have of God, and ye are not your own?" (1Cor. 6:19) The spirit built the body and rules it jealously. Read and meditate Psalm 139, for further insight.

Through self-acceptance or self-love we accept or love ourselves as we are, i.e., as we have been created by our individual spirits. The first and great commandment is therefore to love yourself, by acknowledging your own spirit or god, with all your mind, whole-heartedly.

And the second great commandment is like unto the first: Thou shalt love thy neighbor as thyself. The spirit in you and the spirit in your neighbor are children of the same Universal Spirit. When you accept yourself as your spirit has created you, then you will be able to accept others as their own spirits have created them.

The commandments are thus: (1) Accept and love your personal spirit or god; (2) Extend this acceptance and love to the spirit or god in your neighbor and in all things.

Violation of these great commandments is the unforgivable "sin against the Holy Ghost."

This was well known to the ancients. The Stoics expressed it and taught it in their magnificent philosophy. The Stoics of Rome and of Greece originally expressed it by what they called theocrasy. Theocrasy has a compound meaning—theos, "a god or divine being," and krasis, meaning "an intermingling"—an intermingling of everything in the universe, intermingling with everything else, nothing possibly separable from the rest, the Whole. It is the cardinal heresy of the Oriental religions today, notably in that of the Buddhists, if a man thinks that he is separate or separable from the universe. This is the most fundamental error that man can make. The early Christians called it the "sin against the Holy Ghost." If we look around us and if we look within, we realize that we are one entity, as it were, one great human host, one living tree of human life, woven inseparably into and from nature, the All.

One way of discovering the resident spirit is by "emptying the mind," pouring out the trashy stuff it contains, the illusory beliefs, the false views, the hatreds, suspicions, carelessness, etc. By emptying out all this trash, the temple within is cleansed, and the light from the God within streams forth into the mind. For more on this, see the author's book "The Second Birth. The Mind is a Bag. How Loaded is Yours?" Trafford Publishing.

The God you can know is right there in your body. You need no guru nor complicated yoga stuff to discover It. A realization of Its presence is all you need and the "ahaa!" phenomenon grips you. Let me explain with an example.

When we are asleep:

(a) The blood circulates, the heart beats, the food we ate is digested, our lungs function, the body tissues are repaired, etc. The power in charge of these activities rests only at what we call death. That power is our God!

(b) We cannot think, we cannot express anger or love, etc. The

28

power in charge of these activities is the mind. It tires and rests. It gets its fuel from the power in (a).

If we grasp the above distinction, then we can say "ahaa! is that all?" It is so simple. This mental acceptance of a power that we already have is the first step on the path of knowing our God progressively. And the more we know our God, the more we trust It and are ready to venerate It.

If you fail to find this God within you, then God to you will remain an empty word. And words are not worth fighting for. I am showing you the elephant, not its footprints. But we are free to choose what we want to see: the elephant or its footprints.

What about the government of the world? Since there is mechanical action in the universe, there is government or mechanics at work, producing the movements of the mechanism, in accordance with Divine Plan. In other words, the Gods are behind the Cosmos, spiritual beings, spiritual entities—the name matters nothing. Not God, but Gods.

Nature is imperfect, hence of necessity makes mistakes, because its action derives from hosts of entities at work—what we see around us all the time is proof of it. Nature is not perfect. As mentioned above, the prototype is perfect, but the builders reproducing it are many and diversely talented. As a result, some copies of the original may be defective.

As stated earlier, our objective is to explain Ödïnanï, the Igbo religion. But since the subject would use terms such as religion, God, Gods, Spirit, Spirits, universe, man, etc., it was natural for us to state what we understand by those terms. I stated that it would be dishonest for me to ask someone whether he believed in "God" without first telling him what the word "God" stood for. To assume that he should know, since it is "common knowledge", would be bigotry on my part. The fellow would put me in a tight corner if he had the intelligence to ask me for a definition of my "God", in order to help him decide whether he believed or not in the thing defined. I hope the above clarifications provide ample information to understand what follows. As we shall see, Igbo theogony compares favorably with other known theogonies—Hebrew, Hindu, Orphic, etc.

2
ÖDÏNANÏ OR IGBO RELIGION

GODS ARE THE CREATIVE FASHIONING POWERS

The person who believes in the words and teachings of St. Paul, has no right to pick out from the latter those sentences only that he chooses to accept, to the rejection of others. St. Paul teaches most undeniably the existence of cosmic gods and their presence among us:

(1) "For though there be that are called gods, whether in heaven or in earth, as there be gods many and lords many."(1 Cor. 8:5)

(2) "For by him were all things created, that are in heaven, and that are in earth, visible and invisible, whether they be thrones, or dominions, or principalities, or powers: all things were created by him, and for him." (Col 1:16)

(3) "To the intent that now unto the principalities and powers in heavenly places might be known by the church the manifold wisdom of God" (Eph 3:10)

Gods are the creative fashioning Powers. And the Christian Jehovah is one of the Gods or Elohim. To make of him, as the Christians do, the Infinite, the One and the Eternal God, is philosophically unacceptable. Of tribal Gods there were many; the One Universal Deity is a principle, an abstract Root-Idea which has nothing to do with the unclean work of finite Form. We honor and venerate the Gods as beings superior to ourselves. In this we obey the Mosaic injunction, while Christians disobey their Bible—Missionaries foremost of all. "Thou shalt not revile the gods," says one of them—Jehovah—in Exodus 22:28; but at the same time in Exodus 22:20 it is commanded, "He that sacrificeth to any God, save unto the Lord, he shall be utterly destroyed." Now in the original texts it is not "God" but Elohim—and we challenge contradiction—and Jehovah is one of the Elohim, as proved by his own words in Genesis 3:22, when "the Lord God said: Behold the Man has become **as one of us**," etc. Going by the Christian Bible, both those who worship and sacrifice to the Elohim, the angels, and to Jehovah, those who revile the gods of their fellow-men, are great transgressors.

In every living form resides a manifesting spirit (Chi). All forms—whether stars, men, beasts, or the stones underneath our feet—are tabernacles for spirits (Chi), vital breaths, portions of the same Universal Breath or Spirit (Chineke). And man sees truth when he realizes that he is one-in-spirit with all that is. This realization is the basis of ethics or morality. Without this realization mutual love and brotherhood are just words.

That Chi is key in Igbo theogony is evidenced in such expressions as: Chi na-edu (It is the Chi that guides); Chi m e-gbuo m-oo! (My Chi has abandoned or killed me!); Onye na Chi ya (To everyone his Chi). In these examples the use of Chi is preferred to that of Chukwu or Chineke, because Chi is closer to man than Chineke or Chukwu. The Dibïa Afa always says Kenee Chi gï (Thank your Chi or God) and never Kenee Chukwu/Chineke (Thank Chukwu/Chineke or God). Shielu Chi gï ite! Cook a meal for your Chi! Birthday celebrations are supposed to be Eucharist feasts in honor of the Chi: i-shilu Chi gï ite. Alas, our birthday celebrations are meaningless shows to remember a date.

From the above analyses, we are now able to establish the following table showing the place of Igbo theogony in universal theogony.

Igbo	Universal	Comment
Amaamaamachaamacha, Chukwu	Godhead, Infinite Space	The unmanifest and unknown God, The Great God

Chineke, Mmöö, Ndü	God, Spirit, Life	The manifest, creative God or Spirit
Alüshï, Ndï Mmöö, Chi, Okechukwu	Gods, Spirits	Spirit Guilds, Spirits incarnate in form, Spirit-share
Uche	Mind	Thought is Echiche
Ahü, Arü	Body	
Mmadü	Human Being	
Anï, Ana	Earth, Earth God	The planet on which we live
Obunana (O bu n'Ana)	Earth spirits	Earth God and Its Hosts
Ödïnanï (Ö dï n'Anï)	Earth spirits	Earth God and Its Hosts
Önwa	Moon	
Anyanwü	Sun	
Üwa	World, Solar System	Also the great universe

The awareness of a community is dependent on the awareness of its citizens. Do you know yourself and accept yourself as you are? Only he who accepts himself as he is can accept others as they are. You and I have a Chi or Spirit-share (Oke Chukwu). Your Chi and my Chi were given to us by the manifest creative God (Chineke). Your Chi and my Chi come from the same source (Chukwu), and that is what unites us as children of one God (Ümü Chukwu, Ümü Chineke). Your Chi and my Chi are here on different missions, and that is why we behave differently. This is the foundation stone of the healthy Igbo brotherhood and spirituality.

The Igbo venerate or worship the God of the Earth and Its Hosts of spirits (Anï). Ödïnanï or Omenana describes this method of venerating or worshiping God. Recall that worship of God describes the ways we choose to commune with the manifest God and, through It, with the Godhead (Chukwu)—the Source. Men worship God in diverse, but equivalent, ways. The God is the same—Spirit, Mmöö, Ndü—but the rituals or methods for approaching It differ.

Ödïnanï is the religion or cult dedicated to the Earth God, in the same manner that Christianity is the religion or cult dedicated to the Sun God. Sun Day or Sunday is the day set aside for the Christian worship of the Sun God.

This write-up is a modest gift to Ndï Igbo (the Igbo) aimed at helping them clear up the mental cobwebs that have tried but failed to choke out their religion. Ödïnanï is eternal and unfailing! The song "Omenanï na Üka" by Özöemena Nsugbe should inspire repentance into the Igbo. By repentance I mean a change of mind or a mental purge.

The robust Igbo religion places God in Nature, where Deity is readily available. We are told to embrace the God in us (Chi) so that the latter will embrace the Creative God (Chineke), which already embraces the Great God (Chi-ukwu or Chukwu). Onye öbüna maküö Chi ya, ka Chi anyï wee maküö Chineke bü onye maküü Chukwu. The Earth (Anï) is sacred, keep it holy. Anï dï nsö, debe ya nsö. Anyï na-asö nsö Anï be anyï. May Anï protect man and woman. Anï zöba nwoke na nwaanyï. A mortuary song says that we all belong to the Earth. Anï nwe mmadü niine. Our ancestors knew that the God or Spirit (Chi) of any thing on Earth is subservient to the Spirit or God of the Earth (Chi of Anï = Anï). The latter is subservient to the Spirit of the Sun (Chi of Anyanwü = Anyanwü). By venerating or worshiping Anï our ancestors showed their wisdom concerning the hierarchical structure of the inner government of the world. Those who worship the God whose body is the Sun have put aside a day, Sunday, for Its worship. But this God is the God of the Gods of the planets in our solar system. The inhabitants of Earth have access to the God of the Earth, Anï, and cannot have direct access to the solar God, Anyanwü. Solar religions on Earth have all perished because men have tried to reach the top of a strict hierarchy without going through the basic and intermediary stages. Give unto Caesar what is his, says Jesus. Give Anï Its due and life becomes blissful. The Earth owns us all. Anï nwe mmadü niine!

THE TEMPORARY LOSS OF ÖDÏNANÏ

No pen or tongue will ever record the monstrous fatuity involved in the spectacle of a race looking into the wrong world and waiting with sanctified stupidity for the fulfillment of values that have slipped through their clumsy hands.

The collapse of true religion is ever marked by its turning for its real experience from earth to mystical heavens. When religion gave up its effort to realize values in the life here and fixed despairing eyes on heaven, it signaled the decay of primal human virtue and a sinking back into mystical fetishism. This is the sad fate of Christianity!

Colonialism brought Christianity to Nigeria. With the arrival of Christianity in eastern Nigeria came the Igbo "loss of nerve" and the turning from earth to heaven for the realization of hopes ground to dust on earth. This shift of philosophical view let the ground of Igbo culture lie fallow, and bred the rank growth of religious mummery that has almost covered the whole cultural terrain.

Ödïnanï is the primeval revelation given to early races for the guidance and instruction of all humanity. It is a sobering realization for all of us that this primeval revelation given to early races for the guidance and instruction of all humanity has missed entirely the world for which it was intended!

The scene of critical spiritual transactions is not "over there" in spirit land, but here on Earth in the inner arena of man's mind. Life's accounts do not remain suspended during our active experience on earth, to be closed and settled when the exertion is over. We are weaving the fabric and pattern of our re-creation of ourselves when we are awake on earth, not when we are at repose in ethereal heavens. The droning cry of lugubrious religionism for centuries has been to live life on earth merely as the preparation for heaven. But there is no logic in the idea of making preparation for rest! It is the other way around: rest is a preparation for more work. The positive expression of life is the exertion of effort to achieve progress. Rest is just the cessation of the effort, and needs no preparation. Rest is in some degree correlative with the effort. Still the logic is indefeasible, that we work to achieve our purposes, and not to gain rest. The presumption that this life is of minor consequence and has value only as the stepping-stone to another where true being is alone achieved, is one facet of that enormous fatuity of which we are holding orthodox Christian indoctrination guilty. It is the last mark of the miscarriage of primal truth in the scriptures that its meaning and application have been diverted from that world it was intended to instruct, and projected over into another where its code can have no utility whatever. The offices of religion have fled to heaven, and must be brought back to earth, the scene of the judgment, hell, purgatory and the resurrection, and the seat of all evolutionary experience. This return can be effected only by the retrieval and dissemination of the lost tenets of Nature religion or Ödïnanï.

The colonialist came to the Igbo with his technology and his Christian religion. We should have accepted his technology and politely rejected his ineffectual and mind-warping religion, as did the Chinese and the Japanese. We did not, and this was the Igbo "loss of nerve".

Can the damage be repaired? Yes, since it is entirely mental. Mental garbage can be thrown anytime we realize our error. The mind is a bag, uche bü akpa, into which we have ignorantly stuffed thrash. We simply throw the thrash when, through knowledge, we realize the mistake. My morning starts whenever I wake from my night's sleep. Mgbe onye tetalü n'üla bü utütü ya. Let us mentally go back to our roots in Anï so that It will start protecting us again. Anï ga-ebidokwa zöba anyï!

Is the Igbo a polytheist? Yes, and he is closer the truth about God than the sneering, ignorant monotheist. We saw above that God is both one and many, just like the Army. The Army is a Unit with functional sub-divisions. The same holds true for God. It is one Spirit, one Unit whose functional parts are Gods or Spirits. The functional parts of the Army are hierarchized. The same is true of the Gods. It is meaningless to assert that I applied to the Army for help to put out a fire in my house. The correct statement is that I applied to the Fire Brigade of the Army for help to put out a fire in my house. It is the Fire Brigade of the Army, not the whole Army, which handles fire-fighting. Similarly, we apply for help to a God in charge of a particular function, say, procreation (Akwalï Ömümü). To pray to a God makes sense, but it is foolishness and ignorance to pray to God. To worship or venerate God is inefficacious, but to worship or venerate a God yields immediate results. Our ancestors knew this and that is why they were ö-göö o-lee. Their prayers to a given God always yielded the desired result.

We repeat: Before the advent of Christianity in our midst, the Igbo mindset was that God is both one and many, just like the Army. The Christian mind-warping strategy was to assert that there is only One God, the Christian God, which is the God of all Gods. Man's salvation lay in venerating and worshipping this Christian super-God. But the sober truth is that the Christian God is just one among the many Gods. The attempt to reject the Gods and cling to some super-God unsettles the mind because that mindset goes against all our observations. Can the world in front of our eyes be the creation of one super-God? No!

Nature confirms the reality of Gods or fashioning powers, but not the reality of one super-God.

To get a people under your control in order to exploit them, you must get total control over their bodies and minds. Military might takes care of the physical control. Religious indoctrination with mind-warping dogmas takes care of the mental control, because it destroys whatever mental strength the people draw from their local belief systems. A people thus mollified and rendered docile may be exploited with great ease. This is the ageless, all-time colonization strategy. Ödïnanï was the Igbo religion before the arrival of the colonialists. The observed attempt by our colonial guests to destroy Ödïnanï is simply an application of the ageless colonization strategy: mollify us and render us docile in order to exploit us. The colonialist military might took care of physical control and the job of mental mollification and stultification was given to Christianity, the religion of the colonialist. Ödïnanï had to be sabotaged and destroyed from within. The Igbo woman is responsible for the care and upbringing of children. In wealthy polygamous families the children lived with their mothers in the latter's residences, mkpuke. Christianity recruited the required saboteurs from the womenfolk. Women from wealthy polygamous families were choice recruits for the Christian missionaries. The other fertile ground for the recruitment of saboteurs of Ödïnanï was the group of local underdogs: women who felt crushed by a male-dominated society and men who felt they were unjustly ostracized by a society to which they rightly belonged (Oru, Osu). Oru could be a slave or an indentured servant, and the community has appropriate rites to de-bond those affected. The Osu issue is a bit more complex than that of the Oru. The Osu system was abolished in 1956 by the then Eastern Nigeria government. So, why has the system persisted? Because no one has accurately explained what the Osu is. The explanation below is an attempt to further clarify the Osu concept, with a view to finding lasting solutions to the Osu dilemma. So, what is the Osu?

The Osu is a person owned by the Alüshï. This ownership may be voluntary or involuntary on the part of the Osu.

Voluntary Osu: Faced by some grave danger, a man could take refuge at the shrine of the Alüshï. He thus puts himself and his descendants into the care of the Alüshï.

Involuntary Osu: One may also hand himself over to the Alüshï by deliberately destroying the Alüshï's property. A very Christian lady got into trouble by deliberately smashing the Imöka Awka tortoise with her fufu pestle (ödü nli). Her refusal to perform the propitiation rites transformed all the members of her family into Osu Imöka. There is also the case where two people go before the Alüshï to swear as to the veracity of their ownership claims on, say, a piece of land. The terms of the oath may:

(1)   Limit the action of the Alüshï to the two people who take the oath. Punishment by the Alüshï affects only the oath taker that lied.

(2)   Extend the action of the Alüshï to the descendants of both parties. This option requires the physical presence of the families of the two people when the terms of the oath-taking are spelt out and when the oath is actually taken. So, your family will stand behind you and hold your waist while you are swearing. Ndï be gï ga-amanye gï aka n'ukwu. Punishment by the Alüshï affects the oath taker and those who stood behind him.

Things could get complex depending on the nature of the Alüshï. If the Alüshï is O gbuo ö kpölii mgbo (it kills and takes all property), then the risk is enormous. Some deluded criminals have brought disaster to their folks with this type of oath-taking. They were convinced that their ötümökpö ndagbu iyi (Alüshï neutralizer talisman) would protect them. Alas! The mighty fell and brought untold hardship to their undiscerning folks.

The Osu, his family and property belong to the Alüshï which owns the Osu. By taking a woman from an Osu family without the consent of the Alüshï, one forcefully takes something that belongs to the Alüshï. And that's neither elegant nor wise! Because the Alüshï will go looking for Its stolen property. Onye malü ife ga-ese okwu, nya emekwana ya. If you know that an action will bring trouble, don't do it.

Is the Osu at the shrine a monk? No. The Osu at the shrine is simply a servant of the Alüshï under the superintendence of the Eze Mmöö, who is the gatekeeper of the Gods. Nwaaka-Nrï, not Osu, are the monks from Nrï who cleanse abominations, ï kpü alü.

The Osu label is not indelible. Osu is Ödïnanï-based. The community and Alüshï owners have appropriate rites to straighten out such issues. Those who want to eradicate the Osu system should take a leaf from the above explanation, which provides the reason for the failure of the 1956 legislation to abolish the Osu system in Ana Igbo. In Ödïnanï, the way up is the only way down (ebe e-shi a-lïgo ka e-shi a-lïtu). To ignore this rule is to court disaster and unnecessary trouble. Render to Caesar the things that are Caesar's, says Jesus.

In line with the above, I will now recount the temporary loss, through a woman, of Ödïnani in my family at Ümübeele village, Awka, Nigeria. Our story began circa 1899 when my father was born and is still unfolding. Here it is!

My great-grandfather, Udoh Anaagö, had the Özö title and was the high priest of Anï (Eze Anï) in the Agülü community of Awka. The community comprises the following villages: Ümüönaga, Ümüögbü, Ümübeele, Ümüenechi, Ümüike, Ümüörüka, and Ümüjago. The Anï shrine (Aja Ana, Aja Anï) still exists at the Ümübeele Afö market/village square.

Within his compound at Egbeana Ümübeele, Udoh Anaagö had his Obi (temple), a miniature Anï shrine (Aja Anï), and the following Alüshï or Gods: Agwü, Ngwu, Okuku. Agwü can be mapped into the Greek God Hermes, the wise and wily messenger of the Gods. We note that Anï is the head of the Alüshï. Every prominent Alüshï shrine has its Agwü or messenger. Some families have the Agwü too. In any ögü e-ji öfö (fight for right) the complainant first goes to Anï (Aja Anï) and then to the Alüshï. The Alüshï then sends its Agwü to harass the accused. The tormented accused then consults a Dibïa Afa, who advises him to go to the Alüshï for a settlement. The symbol of Agwü is the Ogilishi tree, while a tree from the acacia family symbolizes Ngwu. Okuku is symbolized by the sacred corked calabash with its mysterious contents. My family's Okuku has three corked and padded calabashes placed in a long oblong basket (ükpa[1]), Öfö, a horn (mpu mgbada) that the priest blows at the close of the Eucharist ritual. Okuku is familiar to the Agbaja people and points to my family's Agbaja ancestry. It belongs to Anaagö Mmadüagwu, Udoh's father. We also have an Akwalï Ömümü, the God of fertility and procreation, but It is located in the Obi at the compound of my great-grandfather's grand-mother, Ashïï Nta Nwüwa Öma, behind Obi Beele Anwünya (Beelu Önwü) at Enugo Ümübeele. Maazï Ödïïkpo, Ashïï's husband, was a wealthy polygamist whose wives lived in secluded compounds (mkpuke) within the larger walled family compound. Members of the Ümü Ashïï clan of Ümübeele village are the direct descendants of Maazï Ödïïkpo through her wife Ashïï.

When Udoh Anaagö passed on his eldest son Anïzöö Udoh, my grand-father, took charge. My grand-mother, Nwaküeri Obilinjö, was one of his three wives (the first!). She was a daughter of the well-known Maazï Oti Anagbögü of Ümüdiöka village, Awka. This woman made history in my family and in Awka. She was tall and very strong. She

---

1   See front cover of this book.

had, as we say, a single bone (ofu ökpükpü) in her arm. In the usual polygamous family brawls, she would floor her two co-wives and sit on them. She had such physical strength that her husband and neighbors could not move her away from the human chair made of her co-wives. My father, Nwabüishi Anïzöö (1899—1964), was her only child. As fate would have it, Anïzöö's other two wives had no male issues. My father, Nwabüishi, was thus the only hope his father had of a successor to take on the symbols of ancestral power, öfö na alö, when he passed on. The Öfö is the wand of power and the Alö is the staff of authority. The Alö is a combination of a spear and a bayonet linked by a common handle. When a son accepts the öfö na alö from his dying (or dead) father, he is duty-bound to take care of the family, its Gods and the Obi where there is one.

Disaster struck my family when my grand-mother, Nwaküeri, got baptized into Christianity by late Reverend Dr. G.T. Basden of the Church Missionary Society (CMS). Her Christian name was Joana. My grandfather was outraged but he kept his cool because of his infant heir, my father, who was Nwaküeri's only child. But my grandmother put a cherry on the cake by showing up in a blouse given to her by the Anglican missionaries, to hide her "nakedness". This was an unpardonable abomination on the part of an Awka woman. In those days maidens walked about naked or with a few rolls of beads (jigida) around the waist, while the married women dressed quite scantily. Nudity was natural to my ancestors until the repressed and vicious missionaries showed up in our midst. Thus did my grandmother become one of the pioneer Christian converts and the first woman to wear a blouse in Awka.

My grandmother got baptized by these white strangers and put on their clothes, without my grandfather's prior approval. Pushed to the wall by his unreflecting wife, my grandfather struck back. He handed her a humiliating separation package. The village assembled in my spacious compound and the men dragged her out into the courtyard. Her legendary physical strength was useless against the men of the village. They would have beaten her into pulp had she attempted to resist them. Arrangements were made by my folks to accompany, to the Öbïbïa River just behind the compound, any of her missionary friends who dared to come to her help. But they wisely stayed away. My grandmother was smeared with charcoal, dressed in rags, dry banana leaves, snail shells, little bells, and what have you. She was transformed into a weird masquerade-like mad person. A big crowd of young men and women made music with drums, gongs, cymbals, and empty tins. With my little father in one hand and a bag of personal effects in the other hand, my grandmother was forced to dance at the head of this curious village brass band. The crowd sprayed her with sand as she danced through the seven villages of Agülü, before proceeding with the musicians to her father's house in Ümüdiöka village. My people handed her and her son over to her bewildered folks. The Oti family and the Ümüdiöka people felt humiliated, but swallowed their pride in the light of the abomination committed by their daughter. The treatment meted out to my grandmother is the famous ö-gba n'ajïlïja (sand spraying) punishment. It is the ultimate in public disgrace. My father grew up with his mother at Ümüdiöka and, with time, uninformed Ümüdiöka people thought he came from their village. He had real bow legs and was a powerful wrestler. He was cool, ruthless and swift like a leopard. His mother's folks have a leopard (agü) cult into which their meritorious sons were initiated. They nicknamed him Ödabalagü Ümüdiöka, probably because he was naturally endowed with the qualities of that big cat without being a member of the leopard (agü) cult.

The CMS missionaries took Nwaküeri and her son to their base at Nteje. My father entered the primary school while his mother received training as a midwife. He later went, at his expense, to the Government Teachers Training College at Warri. The money he earned during school vacation by fishing and trapping bush meat was enough to cater for his school fees and pocket money. His father regularly sent for him, just to see him and know how he was doing. My father moved back to his father's house at Ümübeele before leaving for training at Warri. Life with his father was rough. He cooked for himself in the absence of his mother, since he would not accept anything from his mother's heathen co-wives. His father was busy with his iron works and elephant tusk business. My father's peers at Warri were: Mr. B. Umerah from Ümüenechi village and onetime Headmaster of Government School Awka, where I was a pupil from 1952 to 1956; Mr. Udeözö from Amenyi village whose residence is beside the Nkwö Amenyi market square.

My father was also baptized into Christianity and was given the name Godfrey. But is the name Godfrey actually God-Free or Freed by God? Yes, I would go for Godfrey = Freed by God in the light of what recently happened to him and his mother. My family at Ümübeele was a stronghold of Ödïnanï, which the wily Christian missionaries saw as the Devil's kingdom to be taken by violence. The Christian missionaries deluded my grandmother into believing that her humiliation and divorce was the mighty work of their God, who had freed her and her son from the Devil's lair. Hence the name Godfrey or God-Free given to her son at his baptism. But what the cruel and scheming Christian missionaries failed to tell my grandmother was that she was being used as a potent weapon against her husband's religion, Ödïnanï. By removing the sole male heir to my grandfather, the continuation of Ödïnanï when he passes on was no longer assured. Separated thus from his father, my father had no preparation on how to take care of the family Obi or on how to officiate Eucharist rituals for the ancestors and elders (Ndï Ichie) or the family's Gods (Alüshï). Although he visited his father during his stay at his mother's village (ikwu nne), his mindset and the duration of such visits were inappropriate for meaningful talk on Ödïnanï. His stay with the Christian missionaries had almost stultified his reason and his visits were brief. Knowing his father's ruthlessness, he was careful in his dealings with him. His father was also wary, to avoid losing his sole heir for good. The fact was that he left his father as an infant and came back after college as a complete stranger to the customs of his ancestors. But my grandfather was confident saying that the penis of the warrior never gives birth to a coward, utu dike a-nara a-mü onye üjö. The Obi may kneel down, but it never crumbles, Obi na-egbu ikpele mana ö dï-elu anï.

After his training at Warri, my father got a job as a Government School Teacher. He saved money and, in the early 1920's, spoke to his father about bringing back his mother and getting married thereafter. His father was elated about the marriage idea but gave him two conditions for the return of his mother. The two conditions were:

(1) My grandmother may come back but she will not live in the same house with him. My father proposed to build a brick house in which he will live with his mother, while his father stayed alone in his three-bedroom house. His father agreed.

(2) My grandmother will go through the traditional apology ritual (ï-kü di), ö ga-akü di ya. She will bring a castrated goat (mpïpï), a cock (egbene), eight yams, a Congo bottle of gin (njenje), two gallons of toddy palm wine, a day-old chick to cleanse her with (i ticha arü), kola nuts, alligator pepper (ose örö), ten smoked catfish for prayer (amalü-ile) and for preparing soup for the ritual, sundry soup items. The ritual takes place in the family Obi in the presence of my clansmen. On the appointed ritual day, she just ties a wrapper to cover her body from the breasts down

to the knees and then walks barefoot into the Obi. Kneeling down and facing the sacrificial altar (iru mmöö), she repeats the relevant apologetic phrases pronounced by the officiating elder (priest). The priest then cleanses her by touching her all over with the day-old chick, which is set free thereafter to carry away her sins. The priest then breaks a four-lobed kola nut and asks, before throwing the lobes onto a wooden tray, our ancestors (Ndï Ichie) to indicate their opinion through the pattern displayed by the kola nut lobes thrown onto the wooden tray. The kola nut lobes are then thrown onto the wooden tray and all elders in the Obi are invited to come forward and see the resulting pattern. I was told the ritual went well, so I suppose the four kola nut lobes were all facing up, lying on their broad and flat outer sides. The priest then filled the altar cup (buffalo horn, mpu atü) with palm wine, tasted it, poured some of it onto the altar face and objects (iru mmöö, öfö, okpenshï, ikenga), and gave the cup to my grandmother to drink up whatever remained. The gin came next and a small tumbler or shot was used. After this the members of my clan came and helped her to her feet, embraced her and welcomed her back into the clan. She then left the Obi and my male folks continued the ritual.

A six bedroom bungalow having a large parlor and two verandas was put up. One face of the cement blocks was smooth and the opposite face was decorated with beautiful flower designs. The faces of the blocks with flower designs formed the outer part of the walls, while the smooth faces formed the inward part of the walls. By 1925, the house was roofed with corrugated sheets, the floors were plastered with cement, wooden doors and windows were fixed, but it had no ceiling yet. The house was habitable! And what of the toilets? There was a bath cabin and a pit latrine behind the house. The pit latrine had a wooden seat on top of the small pit entrance. Cute, eh!

My father was now past twenty-four years of age and his father came up with the urgent request for him to get married without further delay. He replied that he needed to seal the new house to keep off owls, snakes, and giant red-head millipedes (esu nwa-ala). My family compound is the last on the Awka-Nibo road before the Öbïbïa River. The dense forest between my compound and the river was home to diverse flora and fauna. Some of the fauna regularly found their way into the compound. His father asked him to leave the visitors from the forest for him to handle and to use the resources for the ceiling to pay the dowry and effect the marriage rites. Asked how he would take care of the forest dwellers, his father told him that the Udoh family had a cult of all the forest dwellers. For the snake (agwö) or the long thing (ife ogonogo), the family had a cult of the long thing (anyï na-eme ife ogonogo), which was part of the greater cult of forest dwellers. The forest and the bordering part of the Öbïbïa River belong to Udoh Anaagö, my great grandfather. That is why the portion of the river spanned by the Awka-Nibo bridge is called Öbïbïa Ezi-Udoh; the square right in front of my family compound belongs to Udoh Anaagö and is called Ezi-Udoh.

Having completed his mother's apology ritual, my father brought her back to occupy and take care of the new house.

In 1931 my father married Josephine Agbömma Ezenwa (1912—2005), one of the daughters of Özö Mmöötoo-anya Ezenwa of Ümüönaga village, Awka, a wealthy business man who lived on the street bearing his name (Ezenwa Street) at the commercial town of Onitsha. She was fair complexioned, pretty and, above all, daughter of a wealthy Ödïnanï-rooted business tycoon. The eagle-eyed Christian missionaries at Onitsha spotted her and the young Agbömma yearned ardently to become a Christian, as the fable goes. The scheming missionaries must have seen the Holy Ghost Fire right on top of her head! She even used to attend church services secretly. It had to be secret because Özö Ezenwa was deep into Ödïnanï, as a visit to his Ümüönaga compound would convince anybody. His richly decorated Obi had no less than four canons (ogbondu). His Agwü is still there although his Christianized descendants are planning to wreak havoc on the remaining relics that show their strong Ödïnanï ancestry.

"Soon after her marriage, Josephine went for training at the Young Women's Christian Association (YWCA) Onitsha. She was trained in domestic and literary arts designed for young Christian women. Thus, young Josephine was well trained and brought up as a virtuous, Christian woman of the Anglican Communion, enjoying a happy, fulfilled married life with her husband Godfrey, with the support of Mrs. Joana Nwaküeri Anïzöba, a famous Christian mother-in-law. Josephine maintained her Christian faith throughout most of her ninety-three years from her teenage till her death."[2] With three ardent Christians (my father, his mother and his wife) planted in the heart of my family—an Ödïnanï stronghold—Christianity was jubilant. With a thoroughly

---

2   Culled from her profile, prepared by two venerable daughters and read at her funeral
     rites in August 2005.

bred Christian couple in full control of my family after the passing on of my grandfather, Ödïnanï would simply die a natural death from sheer neglect. They only had to be patient and visit the farm while the yam matures, ka a na-eje n'ubi ka ji na-aka.

Just before his death in 1944, my grandfather called a meeting to settle the issue of his succession at the head of Udoh's compound. The Obi and all the Alüshï in the compound belonged to seven[3] families, Udoh's children (ndï be Udoh). The rule has been that whoever succeeded an elder inherited the elder's responsibilities to the extended family. My father's refusal to receive the symbols of leadership and power (öfö na alö) from his dying father meant he would lose the right to live in his father's compound. His father would have renounced him before my kinsmen and Ndï Ichie and he would have been thrown out as an outcast. He would be cut from his roots for good. My father was quick to sense the looming disaster. He recalled the trauma he went through because of Christianity and his mother's lack of discernment. And like the reconstituted Nebuchadnezzar[4], "my father's reason returned unto him". He pleaded that he would take the öfö na alö from his father as his sole heir, but that he was ill prepared to assume the incumbent Ödïnanï responsibilities. He reminded my kinsmen that the events that took him away from his roots were not of his making. It was pathetic! A solution was eventually found. He swore before his father, the elders, Ndï Ichie and Obunaana that he will ensure the physical integrity of the compound, Obi and Alüshï. His cousin, Maazï Okoye Nnajide (Afülükwe), was appointed to handle the Ödïnanï aspects of his inheritance. My father's share in contributions for rituals that involved the clan was handled by his cousin using funds left with him by my father. Thus, the great Ödïnanï lamp that Christianity sought to snuff out of existence has remained alight.

As a Government School Teacher, my father served at Issele-Ukwu, Ögwashï-Ukwu and Irrua, all in Delta State; Ajali and Awka in Anambra State; Afikpo in Abïa State. I was born at Ajali in April 1945 and the family visited our Awka home in 1950 during my father's annual leave. I met my grandmother and I still recall her features as if our meeting took place yesterday. Her height and bulk were impressive.

---

3   Eight families with the Mbanugo family that attached itself to the Udoh family.

4   Dan 4:36"At the same time my reason returned unto me; and for the glory of my kingdom, mine honour and brightness returned unto me; and my counsellors and my lords sought unto me; and I was established in my kingdom, and excellent majesty was added unto me."

She was very gentle and kind. My mother was a pygmy beside this unique woman. She smoked a black pipe. She was indeed special and radiated the aura of a quiet force. When I grew up someone told me that my grandmother punished her impertinent co-wives by blocking their doorways with her body, keeping them prisoners in their houses. Recall the incident where she held down her co-wives, coolly sat on them and defied even her husband who tried to intervene. She was summoned by the elders (ümü nna) and forbidden to engage in brawls with her co-wives. But how would she handle her foul-mouthed co-wives who verbally came after her for a yes or a no? Before the ban by the elders she would quietly walk up to the co-wife that looked for her trouble, floored her and sat on her belly. The choking co-wife naturally started wailing for the help of their husband and neighbors. Neighbors, Nwaküeri is killing me ooh! Agbata obi, Nwaküeri e-gbukwee m-oo! With a ban on brawls imposed by the elders, she devised a new and lethal strategy. A co-wife forgets herself and looks for her trouble? Unlike her usual self, she does not react immediately. This nonchalant posture gives the co-wife the false impression that nothing will happen (gïnï ga-eme?); that the sea has dried up (orimili a-tago). But the co-wife is in for an unpleasant surprise. Early the following morning, this co-wife wakes up to find my grandmother sitting coolly in her (the co-wife's) doorway. The co-wife finds herself imprisoned in her own house. She must simply forget about going to the toilets or kitchen until she presents a loud apology to the human wall sitting at her doorway. To call for help from their husband or neighbors made matters worse, because my grandmother considered such appeal as a sign of impertinence. You look for trouble and when you find it you start screaming for help from others. My grandmother passed on in 1951 and was given a grand burial by my family and the Anglican Church. My father wanted to bury her in the family's compound, but the Anglican Church authorities at Awka refused and asked him to seek the permission of their Bishop at Onitsha. My father chartered a vehicle and went to Onitsha to see the Bishop, who turned down his request. Shattered, he came back from Onitsha and watched helplessly as the priests and lay members of the Church prepared to take away the remains of his mother. The muscles of his face twitched uncontrollably but he managed to subdue the sobs that oppressed his voice. He looked with dismay at my kinsmen who could not stop the proceedings, because her mother's corpse was declared "Church property" (ozu üka). They placed the coffin in a pickup van and headed in procession to the Awka Anglican (CMS then) cemetery, the current Awka market at the beginning of Achala Road. Prior to the coming of Christianity burial rites were handled by the children and kinsmen of the deceased.

My father was bewildered by the treatment he got at the hands of his Church friends. Henceforth, he stayed home on Sundays. My mother took us to Church and conducted fastidious early morning prayers at home before we could rise from our mats. We had to kneel with the elbows on the pillow and the butt in the air. I always dozed off in this weird position. She closes the prayer session with "Ka amala nke onye nwe anyï bü Jisus Kraist na mmekö nke ndï-nsö, nönyelü unu mgbe niine mgbe niine" (May the grace of our Lord Jesus Christ and the communion of the Saints be with you all for ever and ever). We reply, "Amen!" Then she adds "Onye öbüna binie ötö!" (Everybody, get up!) And we all rise from our mats and greet her in English "Good morning Maa!" Her name was Maa to all of us. If you had dozed off and slept during the long prayer session and still have your butt in the air when the others had risen to their feet, Maa will give you a good slap on your butt. It was already difficult for me to wake up early in the morning. A jolting slap on my butt for dozing off and sleeping during a prayer session that meant nothing to me was a bit too much for me. I noticed that my father never went to Church with us and never took part in those early morning prayers. I simulated a belly ache on one Sunday and stayed home with my father while the other children left for the Church with my mother. When my father brought Milk of Magnesia for me to drink, I told him the belly ache was gone. Intrigued by the magical recovery, my father gazed into my eyes gently asked me to tell him what was bothering me. I told him I hated being forced to go to Church on Sundays and being woken up early in the morning for my mother's prayer sessions. I told him about the butt-slaps I received from my mother whenever she caught me sleeping at the end of her prayer sessions. I also asked him why he never went to the Church with all of us. What I said startled him. I was just seven years old. He laughed gently and said I could stay home with him on any Sunday that I did not feel like going to the Church. For the early morning prayers, he assured me that nobody would disturb my early-morning sleep, henceforth. On the issue of not going to the Church with all of us, he told me that he had school chores to handle during the weekend and that he was free to go or not to go to Church on Sundays. The explanation sounded reasonable to me, coupled with the relief he gave me about my exemption from morning prayers and Church attendance. Nobody dared to wake me up for prayers the next morning and I happily stayed home with him on the next Sunday. My father never reprimanded my mother in our presence and my mother never said anything out of ken to my father in our presence. I deduced that he had left my mother with very strict instructions on the issues and just kept my cool.

I remember Ajali for some mind-boggling events that marked my life. Government School Teachers had their residences strung together in a given area, away from the indigenes. It was a Sunday. My father had gone out and would be back in the evening. My mother had gone to some meeting involving wives of Teachers. The neighbor's daughter, of my age, came by and we sat and played on the mud bench (ikpo) in the kitchen. I was wearing a khaki jumper and she had a gown. Both of us had no underpants because of our tender age—about two years. We fondled our genitals and I had an erection that intensified as the play proceeded. The door on the compound's fence suddenly burst open. Led by my mother, the teachers' wives strolled into the compound and, passing in front of the kitchen, proceeded to enter our house through the rear door. My playmate and I were now sitting quietly on the mud bench. My mother looked around, found us sitting, and came to the wide kitchen entrance. She beckoned me to stand up and asked: Ö gïnï ka unu na-eme n'ïkaa? (What are both of you doing here?) I said: O nweree! (Nothing!) The other women came and joined her and my playmate's mother was among them. Without any warning, my mother lifted my jumper and, lo! my erection was still there. She hit me on the face and shouted: Ökwa ï-shï na onwere ife unu na-eme! (You said you were doing nothing!) She held up my jumper exposing my erect and vibrating penis for her colleagues to see, saying: Bïakwanü solu m fülü! Nwaa ga-aduwakwa akpa nwamïlï nwa mmadü! (Come and see this with me! This boy will soon perforate the urine sac of someone's child!) My playmate's mother ordered her to go home and wait for her punishment. I could not understand why my stubborn erection was causing so much trouble and why my mother had to show my erect penis to her friends. Humiliated, I sneaked into my father's room and hid under his bed. I was still there when my father came back in the evening. My mother told him about how I vanished into thin air after what happened that morning. It was getting dark and my father went in search of me. Unable to find me with my usual playmates, he came back home. He had searched our house except under his bed. He came into his room and found me huddled up and asleep under his bed. He woke me up and asked me to come out. I was hesitant and he assured me that there would be no more trouble about what happened that morning. I crawled out from under the bed. He helped me clean away the dust on my body and jumper and led me to the parlor. He sat me down and asked me to tell him what happened and I did. I told him everything, from the mutual fondling to the incident created by my mother. Then he asked for why I had gone to hide under his bed. I told him my mother's friends were occupying the parlor and stared at me each time I passed by, as if I had done something wrong. I went under the bed to stay out of their sight. He laughed in his peculiar fashion, without showing his teeth (amu nkpukpuli). He told me it was natural for a man to have an erection and that I should be careful not to get caught with my female playmates. We had dinner together and the incident was forgotten. But this incident strained my relationship with my mother.

Two years later another sex-related incident took place. A much older girl invited me to their farm, close to my house, to help her do some weeding. It was hot and we soon took cover under a small leafy tree, from where we saw people passing along the road without being seen. I jumped up when she touched my genitals and told her I was leaving, because my mother would beat me for allowing anybody to touch my genitals. She chuckled and said: "But your mother is not here. She will not know unless you tell her." She had a point there and I sat down again beside her. She pulled down my shorts, fondled my genitals and I soon had an erection. Shortly after, she was on her knees straddling my thighs. I was amazed to find my hard penis inside her vagina. She noticed my surprise and told me to be calm, that all was fine. Not quite sure where my penis was, I looked down. She leaned backwards to let me see where my penis was. It was warm inside there and I felt her vagina was spasmodically gripping and letting go my penis. She smiled at me and asked me to urinate inside her vagina. I tried with all my force and no urine came. She stood up and asked me to urinate in the grass and I did so without any problem. She stopped me midway and asked me to urinate into her vagina in the same manner. I still had my erection and we resumed our coitus. After sitting on me for a while, she asked me to go ahead and urinate inside her vagina. I strained hard to urinate but no urine came. We separated again and I urinated without problem. We went back to coitus and no urine was forthcoming. We tried many times without success and I just gave up. It was getting late and I had to be at home before six in the evening. We separated, promising to let nobody know what happened. I left the farm first and she found her way home long after I had left. I found my mother and two sisters at the house entrance peeling yam for dinner. I greeted my mother and moved past them toward my room. My senior sister, Margie, asked me: Kedu ibe i-shi a-bata? Where are you coming from? I stopped in my tracks and snapped: Ö-gbasaa gï? Is it any of your business? I went to my room and lay quietly on my bed facing the wall, contemplating my adventure with that girl at the farm. This idea of urinating in her vagina intrigued me and I thought I would try it someday when I grew up and became stronger. My mother came to my room and said: Nkea arü jüchalü gï oyi, udo ö-dïkwa? Ï ga-elikwe añashï? You don't look bright. Are you alright? Won't you have dinner? Still facing the wall, I told her that I was fine and not to bother about dinner. I was not hungry at all. My experience at the farm crushed out any desire for food. I was happy in my little inner world where nobody could reach and start making unnecessary trouble.

The Ajali-Akpü war affected me too. My house was beside the school palm plantation from which emerged blood-stained Ajali men who were wounded in battle. In the morning, Ajali warriors went to Akpu through this palm plantation with machetes, bows, arrows and a few daneguns. They streamed out before dark with their casualties, who bore open and bleeding wounds. Some wailed for their fallen comrades, whose bodies the enemy had taken away.

In 1951, my father was transferred from Ajali Government School to the one at Awka. His specialty was math, which he did everything to get into my dumskull. I attended the Government School with my father, while my sisters Margaret and Ifeyinwa attended St. Paul's Practicing School (PS) which was quite close to our home. Getting to Government School from my Egbeana Ümübeele home was tricky because I had to cross the tarred Enugu-Onitsha road at the Ukwuöjï junction adjacent to the St. Paul's Teacher Training College compound. This tarred Enugu-Onitsha road was known as "wire road," "üzö waya," because of the telephone poles with wire lines, which dotted one side of the road from Enugu through Awka to Onitsha. Although motor vehicles were rare on the road, safety instructions were given at school and home.

My five-year stay in Awka was exciting, instructive and traumatizing. For the exciting part, I fished in the Öbïbïa River with friends, caught giant rats (eyi) with metal traps (mkpakala), and hunted birds and lizards with a rock-propelling catapult (rubber). I learned to prepare a fishing rod: tying a cotton thread around the metal hook (ukpoo), fixing a lead sinker (oze) around the line, passing the thread through a floater (mgba-ama) and tying the thread around a threaded end of a dry, strong bamboo rod. The bamboo rod had to be really dry to provide some protection against the paralyzing discharges from the electric fish (elughelu). The sluggish, pulpy fish with leopard spots looks quite innocuous. But touch it, and your hand will be paralyzed by a powerful electric discharge. Caught by your fish hook, this unique fish obliges you to drop your fishing rod by sending a powerful electric discharge to your arm via the line and the dry fishing rod. With a fresh bamboo rod the shock is devastating. One day, the fish swam past my bathing team in the river. No one saw it but the water around us suddenly became electrified. We scampered out of the water shouting, Ö kwa-nü elughelu-oo! (It's the electric fish!). We all headed for our homes not daring to go back into the river. The size of the fish is irrelevant, since the smallest among them is as lethal as the big ones. Legend has it that the mother of the electric fish armed her children with the ultimate power because of the mistreatment that was the lot of their specie. Mmegbu mmegbu a na-emegbu elughelu ka nne elughelu ji wee-kawaa nwa ya ishi.

The instructive part came from my observations concerning the Ödïnanï rituals conducted in the compound by my kinsmen. The goings-on at the Obi were fascinating. I ran errands for the elders who came to celebrate rituals at the Obi: I bought snuff (ütaba), kola nuts, and gin (njenje) from my grand uncle's wife who lived right behind the Obi. My father had no objections but my mother was dismayed. She sternly warned me not to accept food or drink from those heathens. There were other boys of my age who came with their fathers. We became friends and worked together for the elders, who were pleased to see me among them. I took my share of food and meat in a plate and secretly gave them to my new friends. When I went into the house to wash my oil-stained hands my mother was furious with me, convinced that I had eaten the Devil's food. I assured her that I had tasted nothing and had given my share of the food to the boys who worked with me. My father called me and congratulated me for giving a helping hand to my kinsmen. Unknown to me, he had watched the whole event from his seat beside the verandah window facing the Obi.

An unforgettable event about the Obi was the case of the son of one of our daughters (nwa di-ana) who had only female children from his wife. He consulted a Dibïa Afa on the issue. The Dibïa told him to go for relevant prayers at the Obi of his mother's kinsmen (Obi ikwu nne). He was to request male children, since he already had three in a row, from the Ndï Ichie of his mother's clan. He should go with a cock (egbene), one gallon of toddy palm wine (nkwü enu), a bottle of gin (njenje), eight multi-lobed kola nuts (öjï Igbo), eight yams, smoked catfish (azü ishi) for prayers (amalü-ile) and the ritual soup, and soup materials (ife ofe). The man (nwa di-ana) came on an Eke market day and I opened the Obi to let him deposit the ritual materials he came with. Maazï Okoye Nnajide (Afülükwe), the officiating priest, soon came in to arrange the altar objects (öfö, okpenshï, ikenga, etc.). My kinsmen arrived and the ceremony began. As an errand boy I sat near one of the Obi's two entrances, from where I could hear what was said in the Obi. The priest sat facing the altar. At his left were the items brought by Nwa di-ana, and at his right was a small stool for his assistant. Nwa di-ana was called to the altar and asked to kneel down beside the priest and face the altar. The priest asked him to tell the Ndï Ichie and the clan the object of his visit. Nwa di-ana said he wanted male children, since he has had three females in a row. He had brought a cock, but promised to bring a goat (mpïpï) if his wife gave birth to a male child. Having said why he came, Nwa di-ana was asked to rise and go back to his seat. The priest then took the öfö in his right hand and repeated what Nwa di-ana had requested as well as his promise of a goat, if his prayer was granted. To close his speech, the priest asked: Nwa di-ana, ö kwa nööfü-ee? (Nwa di-ana have I correctly rendered your prayer?) Nwa di-ana replied: e-e oo! (Yes!) The priest called on Ndï Ichie and Ibe anyï (the clan) and said: Ibe anyï-ee, anyï ga-elinu nyabü iwu-oo! (My people, we shall eat the goat promised by Nwa di-ana!) Then everyone shouted: Isee! Ka anyï gölü ka ö ga-ele! (Amen! Our request will materialize!) The ritual then proceeded with the breaking of the kola nut, the palm wine and gin libations, the killing of the cock whose blood was sprinked on the altar door (ïru mmöö) and altar items (öfö, okpenshï, ikenga, etc.) and whose soft feathers were placed on the blood-stained altar items, the cooking of the food and its presentation in front of the altar, the tasting of the food by the priest, the placing of some soup-soaked lumps of food and four small pieces of the cock's gizzard (eke ökükü) on the altar and an altar item (okpenshï), the sharing-out and consumption of the food, the closing prayers (ï gö o-denigwugwu). I had forgotten the whole event when the same Nwa di-ana showed up and wanted an appointment with my clansmen to give them the goat he promised them a year earlier, because his wife has given birth to male twins. He later came with the goat and the usual Obi Eucharist ritual items (a cock, yams, kola nuts, etc.). I told my mother about what happened to the Nwa di-ana. She was full of disdain, saying that it was a coincidence and that only the Christian God can give children. She reprimanded me, a Christian child, for entertaining the thought that the Obi and its carved idols could give children to anybody. This was in 1953 and I was just eight years old. But the same Nwa di-ana came back in 1955 to announce that his wife had given birth again to male twins. I told my mother that her coincidence had happened again and that this Nwa di-ana has had four boys in a row since he came for prayers at the Obi. She was furious and forbade me to tell her about the transactions at the Obi or any Alüshï in the compound. I turned to my father for an explanation of what was happening and told him how my mother denied the possibility of such miracles coming from a heathen Obi. He said the Obi and Alüshï had a lot of powers that he is unable to explain, given his Christian upbringing. By 1960, this Nwa di-ana had eight boys in a row. He was frightened and came to see my people saying that the boys would one day beat him to death (fa ga-eji aka tigbu m). He now wanted some more female children so as to have sons-in-law. My folks laughed and told him to bring a hen (nnekwu) along with the usual items for the Obi Eucharist ritual. The hen shall be used for the sex-reversal ritual that will change the sex of the coming children from male into female. Just as a cock was used to reverse the sex of the coming children from female into male, a hen will now be used to revert back to females. He did as he was told and had three more girls in a row. He had a total of fourteen children, eight boys and six girls.

For the Agwü, I watched the elders trim Its ogilishi tree and drape its trunk with a piece of white cloth. A day-old chick was tied to a nail on the tree trunk. The little bird's leg was tied to the nail with a thread. It chirped and struggled helplessly. We were told that whoever released the chick incurred the wrath of Agwü. It usually died on the tree at the wake of the day following the Agwü celebration.

For the Okuku, we mentioned above that my family has one with three corked and padded calabashes placed in a long oblong basket (ükpa), Öfö, a horn (mpu mgbada) that the priest blows at the close of the Eucharist rituals. Okuku is familiar to the Agbaja people and points to my family's Agbaja ancestry. It belongs to Anaagö Mmadüagwu, Udoh's father. The Okuku ritual takes place in the backyard (azü owele), at the base of a giant iroko tree standing at Anaagö Mmadüagwu's grave. This vast backyard can only be officially accessed through a carved wooden door (mgbo) that opens backwards into the living area of the compound. The area around the iroko tree was regularly cleaned by the wives of Anaagö's sons. As mentioned earlier, Anaagö's compound is the last on the Awka-Nibo road before the Öbïbïa River. It is bounded by a deep gully that runs down to the Öbïbïa River, the Öbïbïa River itself, and a strip of land that stretches from the cassava ponds (mgboko) before the Awka-Nibo Öbïbïa Ezi-Udoh bridge to Okafö Egbunönü Mgbechi's compound wall, to the end of Ümüökam land that has the same southern limits as Mbgechi's compound, to Mmadïka Nwözöbialü Udoh's backyard that contains the giant cotton tree (Akpü Anaagö) and Nwannu spring, to Nwöfö Nwokweghi Udoh's backyard, to Nwammöö Udoh's backyard, to Nnajide Nnabüeze Udoh's backyard, to the backyard of the central compound occupied by Anïzöö and his brother Nweke (Alüshï) Udoh. A carved iroko door at the back of this central compound is the only official entry point into this vast Anaagö's backyard. Anyone entering the land from any other place than this carved wooden door and without permission from the occupants of the central compound exposed himself to great dangers at the hands of the forest people. Any injury sustained in this backyard during unauthorized entry will not heal until the culprit confesses and comes to the Obi in the central compound for a cleansing ritual. I vividly recall the case of Mrs. Nwaadü Önüzulike whose head was nearly severed by the bamboo tree she tried to fell without permission from my father, the head of the central compound. Özö Önüzulike was my father's senior and a member of the Anaagö family. He ought to have known the rule of entry into this land. Why then did he allow his wife to do what she did? Maybe they thought that the sea had dried up, orimili a-tago. She was in hospital fighting against a death that would have followed, if her husband failed to engage the apology and cleansing rituals immediately. My clansmen surrounded him and told him that he was responsible for his wife's mishap and will be held responsible for her death. To complicate matters they reminded him that his brother-in-law, Maazï Nwöfö, was a boss in the terrible Ümüjago Mgbedike cult. No informed and intelligent person would look for the trouble of this quiet but feared man. He was married to my maternal blue-eyed aunt, Nwïnyïnya Nwöfö (nee Ezenwa). Özö Önüzulike and my clansmen hastened up, the necessary apology and cleansing rituals were done at Obi Udoh Anaagö and his wife was discharged from the hospital. She recovered rapidly and life went on as if nothing serious had happened.

Now back to the Okuku ritual. On a ritual day (Eke or Afö), the priest brings out the oblong basket with its numinous contents. The basket is placed on the ground at the foot of the iroko tree, while the Öfö is placed on Ogilishi leaves in front of the basket. The elements used are: a day-old chick (uliom) or a frog (awö) for cleansing (njü-cha) the altar and the contents of the oblong basket, a ram (ebunu), and the usual Eucharist ritual stuff. But the palm wine is of two types: the standard one mixed with some water (akülü mmili) and the special one with no water (a-tü mmili or örü elu ana). This special palm wine is called örü elu ana, because the wine tapper's collecting gourd does not touch the ground when he comes down from the palm tree. In other words, someone waits for the wine tapper (di ochi) at the foot of the palm tree and receives the wine-collecting gourd from him in mid-air while he is still on the tree. Normally, a special order for this palm wine is placed with a reliable tapper and it is more expensive than the standard type. One liter of the special would yield more than ten liters of the standard type. We have wine producing palm trees at our back-yard. A wine tapper usually exploits these trees for a token annual fee and gives us a free gallon of the standard type every fortnight. When the special brew is needed, his collecting gourd is checked to ensure it contains no water before he climbs up a tree. Whatever the tree has yielded will be taken from him in mid-air before he alights from the tree. The wine thus obtained is the unadulterated yield of the palm tree (ife nkwü gbatalü). The special brew is used at the altar, while the standard brew is served to everybody. Strangers and women do not participate in the Okuku celebration. Any edibles remaining at the close of the celebrations are left at the foot of the iroko tree. The officiat-ing priest sounds the antelope horn to end the feast and the men chant while striking buffalo horns against each other (ekwe mpu) and dance around the iroko tree. At the end of the celebrations the priest replaces the öfö and mpu in the basket, which is accompanied to its place on a rack in the Obi. The carved door connecting the central compound to the backyard is closed and bolted. On the day following the ritual, all types of vulture arrive at the foot of the iroko tree to clean up whatever was left there. There were vultures with a bronze ring on one leg. We may note that the vultures generally arrive when the cock and goat are being cleaned in the fire to remove feathers and hair. If they do not come on their own, the priest loudly beckons them to come with the shout "Ükö lïde!" (Vultures come down!), while throwing around a few pieces of meat. They arrive shortly after the calls of the priest.

Their refusal to come indicates that something is wrong with the ceremony. The ceremony could proceed to its close in the hope that the vultures would eventually come before nightfall. If they fail to come at nightfall, the ceremony is repeated after consulting a Dibïa Afa to find out what went wrong. The vultures reappear and descend naturally when the problem is solved and the ceremony is repeated. Legend has it that: a-chüö aja ma shi-afürö udene, ife melü na be mmöö (something is wrong in the spirit world, if the vultures refuse to show up during a sacred ritual). Let us conclude this section by adding that Okuku is the God of justice and valor that scares the warrior into the bush (öchübalü dike öfïa). In the face of injustice inflicted on my clansman by a more powerful person, my clansman will not engage his offender in ruinous confrontations. There will be no physical or legal fights. He is instructed to come home and present his case before the Okuku. The priest and elders use the four-lobed kola nut method to confirm the veracity of his case. If his case is true, he offers an unbroken kola nut to Okuku (i-zefu öjï) and promises to bring a ram after his vindication. Thereafter, news always reached the clan that the injustice had been repaired with appropriate apology from the offender and his folks. The action of the God is swift and thorough. We call It by many names such as: otigbu onye na-etigbu onye sö ya kwü (protector of the weak), nne elughelu (mother of the electric fish), ebi ogwu (the porcupine), agwö a-taghï ata, ö-jüö ödüdü (the snake that hits with its tail when it doesn't bite).

Three events traumatized me during my stay in Awka. The first incident occurred one moonlit evening when my sister, Margie, kneed my genitals because I was rude to her. My mother was sitting a few feet away but she did not see my sister's kick. I gave a sharp scream and fell into epileptic jerks on the sandy floor of the courtyard. My mother rushed to the scene and in her panic, asked my sister what was wrong with me. My sister said she did not know. My father came out too. Then my breath came back with an excruciating pain in my genitals. I wailed loudly in a staccato. I was fanned with a hand fan (nkucha, nkuufele) and I gradually regained my wits. Then my father asked me what was wrong and I said: Margie gbalü m ikpele n'amü (Margie kneed my genitals). She tried to justify her act by saying that I was rude to her. Before she could finish, my father's folded fist landed on her head (i-ke ökpö) and she started weeping. My father thundered: Shut up! And like magic, Margie stopped weeping. He ordered her to stay away from me or face his legendary cane whip. We all went to sleep and the pain was gone by the end of the following day. The event shocked me, because I thought I was going to die. In retrospect I can now understand how an accident forces the spirit or wind out of the body.

The second incident happened when I stole a sixpence coin (shishii) from under my mother's pillow. I had raised the pillow and found many coins underneath. I took the sixpence coin which was the smallest in size. I bought a few sweets and chewing gum that I shared with my playmates. My mother noticed that a sixpence coin was missing from her treasury. She confirmed with my sisters Margie and Ify that they had no hand in it. She hid a whip under her mat on the mud bed in our kitchen's veranda and waited for my return after dark. The doors from the veranda to the kitchen and adjoining rooms were locked. My father was absent from the house. As soon as I came in and was walking to my room, Margie called me to come and see Maa in the veranda. I went in and as I walked toward her on the mud bed, Margie locked the veranda door behind me. My mother said: Ï welü shishii n'ishi akwa m? Did you take a sixpence coin from under my pillow? I kept quiet. She added: A-gara m eti gï ife ma ï gwa m ezi okwu. You will not be punished, if you tell me the truth. I confessed that I had taken the smallest of the coins under her pillow to buy candy and chewing gum. She grabbed me with her left had and brought out the whip from under her mat. She rained strokes of the cane on me as we ran around the narrow veranda. There was no road for escape since all the doors leading out from the veranda were locked and Margie blocked the veranda's small window with her body. The flogging went on until the cane split in shreds, one of which got into my left eye. I fell on the floor holding my left eye and shouting anya m-oo! anya m-oo! (my eye! my eye!). Sister Margie shouted: gba-kwïa nkïtï, ö mü üma eme ka i wee-rafü ya! Don't mind him, he is pretending so that you will stop flogging him! The cane was completely shredded and broken by now. She left me on the floor and went back to the mud bed. I opened the veranda door, went outside, washed my face and went to my room. My left eye smarted at my touch and I fell asleep exhausted. The next day was Saturday and my mother left early for Onitsha. My sister, Ifeyi, was the only one around. My father asked her about me and she said I was, quite unlike me, still sleeping. I had bolted the door from my room to the veranda where my father sits. He came into my room through my mother's room and found me under my blanket shivering and groaning (na-asü ude na-ama jijiji). He turned me round and could not believe what he saw—my left eye was closed and swollen. He asked: Kedu onye melü gï ifea? Who did this to you? I said: Ö-ö Maa! It was my mother! He summoned my sister, Ify, and asked her to run to Ezi Ekweelu on the Awka-Onitsha road and tell our mother to cancel her trip and come home immediately. Ify left and my father came back to my bed and sat beside me. He asked for the reason why my mother had injured me so badly last night and left me for Onitsha without any care whatever. I told him I had stolen her sixpence coin and confessed to the crime when she had promised no punishment, if I told her the truth. He was furious and asked: maka shishii ka e ji ghülü mmadü anya? How could anybody pluck someone's eye because of a sixpence coin? He gave me some aspirin and mopped my swollen eye with a towel soaked in cold water. Ifeyi soon came back and reported that my mother had left for Onitsha before she got to the bus stop at Ezi Fkweelu. My mother came back in the evening and my father took her straight into his room. We heard nothing as usual, but my mother looked shaken when she came out. She later came into my room and tried to mend fences but I remained cold. My father's words came to my mind: maka shishii ka e ji ghülü mmadü anya? Something snapped inside me and I saw my mother as some cruel Nanny employed by my father to look after us. She never hit me again after this incident. I procured a pebble catapult (egbe mkpume, rubber) and told my father that anyone who injures me again will lose an eye through a pebble from my catapult.

The third incident was a mistreatment, in 1956, by Mr. B. Umerah, my godfather and Headmaster of Government School, Awka. I was ten years old and in Standard 5. We had ended a meeting of teachers and students. We stood in rows, grouped by class. Mr. Umerah asked us to close our eyes for prayers and had said a few words when I screamed because a bully, Lawrence Anekwe, had hit me hard with a whip. I was standing in the back row beside Lawrence, who was twice my age and for which we made fun of him. The Headmaster stopped praying and ordered whoever had screamed to come forward. I moved forward showing him the whip that Lawrence had dropped after hitting me, and told him that I had screamed because the bully flogged me with the whip. He asked me to give him the whip. He then grabbed my hand, took the whip from me and gave me not less than twelve lashes all over my body. He thundered that I had no business disrupting his prayer session with my stupid scream. The teachers and students were scandalized by what happened. My father was there but just watched what was happening. The injustice shown to me by this man was incomprehensible. I was hurt by a bully right in front of this Headmaster and he does nothing to reprimand the culprit. Instead, he gives me, the victim, a severe flogging. The world must be upside down, I thought. I wailed loudly, rained insults on him, opened my ten fingers towards him and said "waka". When my father came home in the evening, I asked him why he did or said nothing to protect me from such a wicked man. He said that he could not intervene, because the man was his boss and could have used that incident to lure him into a conflict that might cost him his position. He said that he had a hard talk with the Headmaster and assured me that a repeat of such an incident, in or out of his presence, was, henceforth, impossible.

My father stayed in Awka till the end of 1956 when he was transferred, as Headmaster, to Government School Afikpo. Life in Afikpo was full of surprises. The town is full of gravel and it was excruciating in the beginning to walk barefoot. We lived on the school campus, situated on a hill along a gravel road leading to the Catholic Mater Hospital. The teachers lived in houses built around the classrooms. The school had a farm and palm plantation behind the Headmaster's house. We fetched water from a superb spring in a deep valley behind the Magistrate Court. From the spring, gravel paths led uphill to the Police Station by the right and straight-on to Number Two, a quarter for non-indigenes. The prison yard, prison staff quarters, residences for civil servants were all at Number Two. The Government College was located behind Number Two and the District Officer's (D.O) residence.

I was impressed by the inter-village wrestling contests and went to watch them at the Ngodo village, which was close to my home on the school campus. Some of my classmates wrestled in the junior category. A winner in a contest was carried shoulder high by his village folk and bare-breasted damsels wearing rolls of beads around the waist as sole clothing, danced to glorify his victory. Wrestling is an art for these great people. I got into a brawl at school with an Afikpo boy of my age. A crowd of pupils gathered around us. I had superior boxing skills acquired from gang brawls back at Awka, while my opponent was a good wrestler. He floored me twice at the start, but I kept him at bay with jabs on the face and never allowed him to get a grip on me. One of my jabs cut his lip and he was spitting blood. My father, the Headmaster, suddenly showed up. The big boys came and separated us, and we were asked to state how the fight came about. Each person gave his version of the events. My father sternly reprimanded us, reminding us that fighting was forbidden in the school. To reconcile us he ordered us to entertain those present with a wrestling contest.

I was dismayed because my opponent had a superior knowledge in the wrestling art, although he was of my age. I managed to put on a brave face and moved into the circle of spectators. He put out his hands, stooping slightly, to engage me. I took the same posture, in line with the rules of the art, and moved towards him. With a swift movement, he seized my hand and forcefully drew me to himself. Feeling the resistance in my counter-pull, he pushed me back and let go his grip. My counter-pull and his push worked like magic. I fell backwards and landed on my butt. The crowd roared with laughter. We were allowed a second contest, probably in the hope that I could win it and get even with my classmate. Intent on not letting him get hold of my hands, I raised them so high that he was able to get hold of my torso, with his arms under my armpits. Before I could figure out what was up, he folded his left leg around my right leg and, still holding my torso, lifted our entwined legs from the ground pushing slightly in my direction. I simply crumbled to the ground with my opponent on top of me. I was thoroughly humbled and my father stopped the contest. I embraced my opponent and shook his hand as my father ordered and we became good friends thereafter. He later taught me the two wrestling techniques he used against me. He made me promise never to use the leg-twining technique outside a sandy arena, to avoid breaking someone's arm in the unavoidable fall associated with the irresistible technique. He observed that a victim of the technique tries to cushion his fall with the arm. A fracture might result when both wrestlers fall together on the cushioning arm.

My indigenous classmates officially stayed away from school during the harmartan months of January and February, to participate in the initiatory masquerade and passage rites (Ogo). The Afikpo boy became a man only after the rites. He had access to the spirit temple (Obi Ogo) at the village square and could take a wife when he became an adult. We sometimes came across our classmates undergoing the initiation. Their only clothing was a loincloth covering the genitals in front and most of the butt at the back. They moved silently in a single file, one behind the other. They had walking sticks with swollen ends with which they struck the ground when they walked along the road. Women moving around during the initiation months chanted "leee, leee" to signal their presence to the student-initiates. On hearing the women's chant, the students leave the road and hide in the bush or behind some house. They come back to the road to continue their trip when the women have passed them by. I was told they are forbidden to come face to face with women, to avoid the situation where a boy meets his mother or sisters along the road. The boy undergoing initiation can have contact with his family only at the end of his stay at the initiation camp. He belongs to his community during his stay at the initiation camp. If he dies during the rite, he will be quietly buried without ceremony and a bunch of the tender yellow palm leaves (ömü) are deposited at the back of his father's house. His mother checks the back of her house daily to see whether the portent had been deposited there the previous night. If she finds the dreaded palm leaves, she does not weep to the hearing of neighbors. When asked about her son, absent from home long after the end of the initiation period, she says he has gone to Panya (Fernando Po, Espagna).

In 1957 I failed the West African School Leaving Certificate examinations. As a result, I could not take secondary school entrance examinations. One of the teachers, Mr. Okonkwo from Ajalï, took charge of my studies and I made a distinction at my second go at the examinations in 1958. In 1959, I took and passed the entrance examinations for: King's College, Lagos; Government College, Afikpo; Merchants of Light Secondary School, Öba; Okongwu Memorial Grammar School, Nnewi; Okuku Boys High School, Obudu. For the interviews, there was none for Okuku Boys High School because I was admitted right at the entrance examination hall. White Catholic reverend fathers invigilated the examinations at the Catholic Primary School opposite Mater Hospital, Afikpo. A Mathematics test came first at eight o'clock in the morning and we had two hours for the test. About an hour into the test, one of the fathers came and stood by my side and watched me answering the questions. I looked up at him and he smiled and walked away towards the table behind which sat another elderly father. I continued writing and finished well ahead of the allotted time. I checked my answers again and proceeded to submit my write-up. The elderly father looked at my write-up and asked me to go home and inform my parents that I have been admitted into the school. He said it was unnecessary to wait for the English test, since my performance in the Math test was sufficient proof of my ability to enter the best secondary schools around. My admission letter was to follow shortly through the post. I went home and told my parents what happened. My mother was indignant about the idea of her CMS-born son attending a Catholic school. She was sure I would come back the next vacation as a baptized Catholic. I had secretly attended a Catholic Candlemass with the sons of Mr. Onyemenam, a Government Teacher from Obosi, whose son,

Ephraim, was a pioneer first-year student at Okuku Boys High School. But for the intervention of Mrs. Onyemenam, I would have taken the Eucharist wafer when the congregation singly walked up to the priest and opened their hand or mouth to receive the blessed wine-soaked wafer. She warned me not to leave my seat and charged her sons to make sure I did not move. I could not understand why she was so worried and tense. The Mass was exquisite: the odor of burning incense, the array of big and small candles, the chanting of the priest and the songs of the reverend sisters that gave me goose-bumps. I thought the communion wafer was some candy to fortify the congregation during this special Mass that started at midnight and ended around six o'clock the next morning. The attitude of this woman disgusted me and I just went outside and sat with people under a tree in the Church courtyard. It was late in the night and I could not go home alone. When the day broke I joined the group of mass attendants going towards the Government School campus. I got home, sneaked into my room and fell asleep. I was woken by Mrs. Onyemenam's voice lamenting my disappearance from their company at the night Mass. My father came into my room through the door linking our rooms, confirmed that I was fine and left. Mrs. Onyemenam was very upset that I had ventured to eat the Eucharist wafer and warned that I should avoid her children and never come to her Church again. It was okay for me and I stuck to her injunctions. If she crossed my path I would mumble a greeting and move on. I had to greet her because she was a good friend of my mother and could create unnecessary trouble for me. If I saw her coming to our house, I would go bird-hunting with my catapult in the palm plantation beyond our backyard. We shall have more on this lady later, because she will play a cruel and terrifying role in my life.

For its interview, King's College sent a letter proposing the sleeper-class roundtrip train ticket from Afikpo Road railway station to Lagos. My mother turned it down on the grounds that Lagos would simply destroy her rascal of a son. She pointed to my two sisters who were at Queen's College Lagos and attended immoral unchristian ballroom dance parties, where unmarried men and women shamelessly fondled each other, and practiced wanton fornication. She insisted I should go to Government College, Afikpo, which was close by, for her to have an eye on me. She added that Government College, just as King's College, offered the same scholarship to the children of Government Teachers. To put the issue to rest, she said that the Government College Principal's wife, Mrs. Mboto, was her friend and member of their

Association of Government Teachers' Wives. She would talk to her if necessary, since my father had warned that he would not lift the smallest finger to push his children into school or job. His father never intervened for him when he was young, why would he do such a degrading thing as going to beg a favor from a man like himself. If a child cannot make it through competition with his peers, let that child stay at home until he is able to make it. It was thus agreed that I should just relax, study and attend the Government College interview. Why go to Lagos to get a thing that is also available on the shelf in front of us? A na-achö ife dï n'uko anï n'uko enu? A co-pupil, Sunday Akpabio, living next door with his Teacher-uncle, left to Lagos for the interview. On his return, he told me of his train journey from Afikpo Road railway station through Kafanchan, Zaria, Jebba to Lagos and his stay at King's College. He later got his admission letter with the offer of a scholarship and he entered King's College at the beginning of January 1960. I went for the interview at Government College campus where we spent two weeks learning boarding house habits and table manners, particularly eating with a fork and a knife. I was startled to see the students eating rice with a fork and a knife. I thought it was some sort of subtle punishment to force anyone to eat rice with a fork and a knife. Getting the rice together to stay on the fork was already a feat. And getting the rice-loaded fork into the mouth was a greater feat, since most of the rice fell back into the plate. Dropping the knife and eating the rice with only the fork was also forbidden. Even the chicken wing served with the rice must also be eaten with the fork and knife. Many of us found our chicken parts, in a bid to escape the fork and knife assault, flying onto the top of the dinning table or the dinning hall floor. Eating with the fingers was out of question and punishable. For the interview proper, we had an individual chat with the Principal in his office. He asked about my parents and how I was getting ready to come to his school. He complimented me for my entrance examination results and bade me goodbye with greetings to my parents. He said the admission letter would follow through the post. I went to the dormitory where I stayed with other would-be students, collected my belongings and walked home. I told my father about what happened during the two-week stay at the Government College campus for the interview. He was satisfied and we all relaxed and waited for the arrival of my admission letter through the post.

Concerning the interview for Merchants of Light Secondary School, Öba, my mother said there was no need to bother about the school, because my elder brother Emeke attended the same school and had dev-ilish encounters with some students. She said some students from Öba had deadly talismans and charms (ajö ögwü) that they used against fellow students. Lightning had struck a dormitory and killed a student from Öba, in whose locker was found a powerful charm. A general search revealed that almost all the students from Öba had some charm in their lockers or suitcases. She was happy that Emeke finished his studies and came out of the school in one piece. I was her second boy and nothing would make her support sending me to that Devil's kin-dergarten, where children manipulated charms that adults feared to touch. Thus was my going to Öba laid to rest.

It remained the interview for Okongwu Memorial Grammar School (OMGS), Nnewi. Eight days before the OMGS interview date, I had no news from Government College, Afikpo. Worried, I went to my fa-ther and told him: "All my classmates who attended the Government College interview with me have received their letters of admission. I have not received mine and I am scared. What would happen if the Government College disappointed me and I failed to attend the OMGS interview just around the corner?" My mother was summoned and asked to find out from her friend, Mrs. Mboto, the wife of the Principal of Government College, why I had not received my letter of admission, while my classmates who attended the same interview with me had all got their letters. She met Mrs. Mboto, who told her to come back after four days, to give her time to find out what happened from her hus-band. My mother went back after four days and came back with sad news. My admission was cancelled after Mrs. Onyemenam paid the Principal, Mr. Mboto, a courtesy visit to discuss the wisdom behind the idea of admitting me into his prestigious school. Mrs. Onyemenam presented me as a Devil incarnate that would irretrievably stain the reputation of Government College, Afikpo. The frightened and God fearing Mr. Mboto yielded to Mrs. Onyemenam's wicked machina-tion against a child of fourteen. And this woman had many children! I can recall her male children: Francis (the photographer), Ephraim, Cyril and Oli. I had promised to come back to this woman, because she marked me mentally. Here she was, her hideous face unmasked! I went to my room, bolted my door and sobbed bitterly. My father was speechless. He joined me through the door between our rooms, sat be-side me on the bed and told me that men rarely shed tears. He said that at fourteen years, a boy has become a man and should cultivate manly attitudes. He asked me to forgive Mrs. Onyemenam and retain the lesson that people wear false faces and are not what they seem. He told me to get ready and leave the next day for the interview at OMGS. His words woke me from my torpor. I looked at his face and said Yessa! (Yes Sir!) We addressed my father as Papa, but used Sir to address him when he asked questions or gave instructions.

As agreed, I left Afikpo by road for Nnewi in the evening of the next day. The journey lasted the whole night with an Onitsha-made tinker bus driven by a stout, fair-skinned and bearded man nicknamed Uduaghïrïgha. The bus had a long snout (iru munchi) which housed the engine and the large cabin for the driver, his conductor and passengers was nicely crafted by the famous Onitsha-based Obiefuna and Sons. It had two exits, one in front opposite the driver's seat and the other on the same side towards the back of the bus. We left Afikpo around seven o'clock in the evening and the journey took us to Okigwe, Isiekenesii, Amaraku, Ekwulobia, Awka Etiti, and Nnobi. We hit Nkwö Nnewi at five o'clock in the morning. Since I had to go back the next day with the same bus, the kind driver personally told me to be present at the spot where I stood, before five o'clock the next morning. The bus would take me to Onitsha to collect passengers and then come back to Nnewi and continue to Afikpo. It was the only bus linking Afikpo to Onitsha every two days. The road from Afikpo to Nkwö Nnewi met the tarred Onitsha-Owerri road at the Nkwö Nnewi junction facing the Post Office. I had dust all over my body and looked like someone dug out of a heap of ash (onye a-võtalü na ntü). My bag-like cane basket contained my small tinker school-box, whose sole contents were two pens, a khaki shorts and a beige short-sleeved shirt. I had no shoes. To reach OMGS, a trader who was opening his shop told me to follow the tarred road in the direction of Owerri. He added that the school was on the right side of the road, not far from the Nkwö market. The day was breaking fast and my interview was at nine o'clock that morning. I took off in a trot and soon reached the Otolo-Ümüdim junction close to Odumegwu Ojukwu's compound. I stopped to catch my breath and a compassionate old man inquired where I was running to with all the dust that covered me from head to toe. I told him I had an interview at nine o'clock that morning at OMGS, and had no idea where to find the school. He confirmed it was along the road, but about two kilometers from where we stood. He asked me to go down to the stream at the bottom of the sloping tarred road and continue uphill on the opposite slope. At the end of this slope was OMGS with an imposing signpost in front of the school compound. I quickly located the school's secretariat.

I told the male secretary that I had come for the interview straight from Afikpo and showed him my letter of invitation. He said I looked awful and asked if I had some clothes to change the dusty ones on me. I told him I had a clean shirt and a pair of khaki shorts, which happened to be the school's class uniform. He gave me a jug of water to wash my legs, hands, face and head. I quickly changed there in everyone's sight, stuck my dirty clothes into my tinker box, and went off with the secretary to the Principal's house a short distance up the road. There were only two students remaining on the interview queue. I sat with them and the secretary went into the Principal's office. He later came out and told me to relax and wait for my turn with Mr. Evans, the Principal. I went in when my turn came and the gentle white man gave me a seat opposite him across a big table. We talked about my father's profession and my family. He then showed me paper cuttings which, when correctly assembled, formed a circular pie. He said I should watch him assemble the scattered pieces and create the pie. He did this twice, scattered the pieces, and asked me to create the pie. To his surprise, I quickly recreated the pie. He scattered them again and, with the same ease, I recreated the pie. He was delighted and told me that I have been admitted to OMGS. He sent for the secretary and asked him to prepare my admission letter for his signature. By four o'clock in the afternoon, I had an envelope for my father containing the admission letter, the list of books for the first year, the list of clothes and shoes (a pair of canvas shoes and white socks, a pair of Bata shoes and sandals, some pairs of stockings). I thanked the secretary for his kindness and set off on foot again back to Nkwö Nnewi to catch my bus the next morning. At Nkwö Nnewi, I quickly identified the trader that I met at five o'clock in the morning when I came down from my bus. Quite cleaned up now, the man did not recognize me until I told him of our encounter that morning. He was delighted that my interview had gone well and gave me a bench to sit down. He sold me a sixpence loaf of bread and that was my first meal since I left home. I had refused to take any food or drink for fear of having to go into the bush to ease myself when the bus stopped for those who wanted to ease themselves. I was fine; the anxiety created by my ordeal took care of the need to ease myself. Soon it was dark and the kind trader invited me to his place promising to make sure I caught my bus at five o'clock the next morning. I thanked him for the offer which I politely declined. I begged him to let me sleep on the bench he had offered me earlier, to ensure that I would not miss my bus which stopped right in front of his shop. He said it was risky because of mad people (ndï ala) that sleep in the market and night marauders (abanï dï egwu). I was undeterred and he agreed. I sat up most of the night and the few people who came around bolted away when they came too close and heard a boy's voice cooling asking them what they wanted. Worried about my safety, the kind shop owner came around four o'clock in the morning and was happy to find me in good health. He gave me a mug of water from his shop to wash my face and clean my mouth. He kept me company until my bus arrived at five o'clock. He took my basket, led me to the bus and bade me safe journey. The bus left Nnewi for Onitsha to collect passengers and goods for the return journey to Afikpo. We left Onitsha late in the afternoon, got to Nkwö Nnewi around six in the evening and proceeded to Okigwe and Afikpo. We got to Afikpo early the next day. I told my parents what had happened and they were happy. My father had his annual leave in December 1959 and the family traveled to Awka, from where I took off to OMGS in January 1960.

Life at OMGS was rough from day one. There were six dormitories going from House A for ruffians to House F for lambs. Each student had a kerosene lamp. From the tarred road, we had House A followed by the Assembly Hall, then came Houses B-D in a straight line, then the dinning hall stood across the space between Houses D and E, facing the direction of the tarred road, and House F came after House E on the same straight line. The two long non-partitioned bathrooms and the bucket latrine cabins were behind House D, as well as the footpath leading down a steep hill to a beautiful spring at the foot of the hill. House A later became Ojukwu House. Each House had two compartments. The large outer compartment was an open hall for students in Classes 1-4. The small compartment was for the House Prefect and Class 5 students. The Class 4 students resided in cubicles at the four corners of the large outer compartment, while the Prefect and his Class 5 colleagues occupied cubicles in the small compartment. The day started at five in the morning with Christian prayers and song from a hymn book, all under the supervision of the House Provost. The House Prefect showed up only when he had some message for all. Water fetching from the spring was shared out among Classes 1-4 students. Class 5 students had errand boys from Class 1 who fetched water for them and the school had a laundry service. Students marked their initials on their clothing with indelible Kandahar ink for ease of identification at the laundry tray. The breakfast bell sounds at seven in the morning and late comers are locked out and their food shared out (massacred!)

to those present in the dining hall. The same fate befalls the food of those who go late for the afternoon and evening meals. Classes began at eight in the morning and ended at two in the afternoon. Late afternoon was used for sports, water fetching and other chores. Evening studies (Prep) came after diner, followed by prayers at the assembly hall and the lights were put out at twenty-one hours. I learned to carry three buckets full of water at the same time: one on the head and one in each hand. I dropped one bucket at the dining hall tank, used one for my bath and kept one under my bed as drinking water.

I met despicable as well as wonderful people at OMGS. The wonderful ones that I recall are: Lawrence Onyewuenyi, my House Prefect and a just man who detested bullies and protected weak students; Önüöra Achukwu of the Achukwu Ochanja family, Onitsha, owners of Achukwu Hall near the Denis Memorial Grammar School (DMGS) roundabout; Emma Obierika; Fabian Okeke; Üba Okonkwo (Kano), a quiet genius; David Enemchukwu, the boxer and defender of the weak. The despicable ones were sexual perverts who sodomized weak students who were unable to bear the infernal rhythm imposed by the powers that be at OMGS. Sodomy was called the Vaseline Experiment. Some teachers, Prefects and Classes 4-5 students transformed weak students into sex slaves in return for protection from harassment. If you refuse to yield to these fellows, you might spend all your time doing unwarrantable chores and punishment for imaginary offenses cooked up by a senior student or Prefect. Some Prefect would storm into the dinning hall, pick up and ring the bell. Before you are able to put down the fork and knife in your hands, he is already pointing at you to mount on your seat. Before you say anything he thunders and punishes you to wash all the dinning plates used by the students from your House. The punishment has no basis whatever and is simply intended to break the victim and send him on his knees to the all-powerful Prefect. When the victim meets the Prefect and accepts to be one of his sex slaves, the punishment is nullified. The first year students have no protection whatever against this abuse. To whom would the victim complain? Everyone in a position of power—the teachers, Prefects and students above Class 1—seem to be participants in this sordid business. I once complained to a Prefect from Awka Province that a Class 4 student was sexually harassing me. He called the student and warned him to stay away from me. But the savior Prefect turned around to ask me for the same business for which he had chastised my Class 4 tormentor. I told him I'd rather leave their rotten school than do such a degrading thing.

The injustice I saw around me and suffered came to a head in March 1963, when the Library Prefect seized my lamp for reading after lights out in a vacant Class 5 student's cubicle. I lost three months of classes after my father's road accident and hospitalization. I stayed home to take care of my little sister and brother while my mother was in the hospital with my father. On my return to school I had to catch up with a backlog of lessons using the notes of my classmates. The only time I could get their notes was at night when they were not using them. My House Prefect saw my plight and gave me the unoccupied Class 5 cubicle for the purpose. He promised to cover me if any Prefect showed up to check those who had their lights on after the lights-out bell. The Library Prefect was adamant to the explanations given by his colleague. He grabbed my lamp and left. At breakfast he stormed into the dinning hall and ordered me to wash the plates used by all the students in the school. My House Prefect did nothing to help me and my brakes snapped. I simply walked to the dormitory and lay prostrate on my bed. By lunchtime the plates remained unwashed, provoking a crisis: the students had no plates to eat with. During Prep classes that night, I went to the Library and told the Prefect that the Senior Housemaster, Mr. Efobi, wanted to see the two of us immediately. The Senior Housemaster lived opposite the school just across the tarred road. The Prefect followed me and I mugged him just in front of House A. After a hammer-blow at the back of his head, he screamed, ran a few meters from me and collapsed. I threw the hammer into a bush near the carpentry workshop, from where I had taken it. I quietly walked into my dormitory, packed my belongings and waited for the worst. When students rushed out to see what was going on, I was lying quietly on my bed. Mr. Prior, the Principal, brought his car and they rushed the unconscious Prefect to Onitsha. When he was revived, he recounted what happened. The students were summoned to the assembly hall where I was summarily dismissed from the school. In addition I was condemned to come back and repeat Class 4. I quietly walked out on everybody, went to my corner, took my belongings and left for my home at Awka. I told my father what happened and mentioned my decision never to go to a boarding school again. He said I should go into my room and get some rest, while we awaited the return of my mother who was absent. We had a meeting when she came back and I was asked about what I intended to do. I replied that schooling was over and I was going to become a motor vehicle mechanic. My friend at OMGS, Önüöra Achukwu, had finished the year before and was running his mechanic workshop at Onitsha. My mother was distressed at the idea that I would not go to the university like my senior brother who was at the Enugu College of Science and Technology. I left for Onitsha and discussed my decision to become a mechanic with Önüöra. He agreed and obtained the okay of his father, Achukwu Öchanja. I stayed with Önüöra and his junior brother, Bomboy, who was also working at Önüöra's workshop. Two months after leaving home, my mother came to see me at Onitsha. I was at the workshop, but she met Mr. Achukwu, Önüöra's father. On our return from the workshop, Mr. Achukwu called me and told me about my mother's visit. He said my mother had wept and begged him to send me back home, where she had got admission for me into Igwebuike Grammar School (IGS), Awka. Mr. Achukwu pleaded with me to go home and come back after completing my secondary school education, to continue my training to become an auto mechanic. I left for home and went to see the Principal of IGS. This was in early August 1963 and the school year was more than half-spent. Here is the deal that the IGS Principal had for me: Class 4, into which I was admitted was already full and I was to attend classes as a clandestine student. If a school inspector was around, I should escape from the class and school compound. If I passed the year-end examinations, I would move on to Class 5. If I failed, then I could come back and repeat Class 4 the following year. To reject this proposal would have hurt my parents, particularly my father who was sick. It was also better than the unique option of repeating Class 4, if ever I chose to go back to OMGS, Nnewi. It was no small challenge, because I had just three months to assimilate the Class 4 syllabus. I thanked the Principal, Mr. Ekwoanya, and walked home. I told my parents that the deal was fine with me and that my brilliant passage to Class 5 would vindicate me concerning the sad events at OMGS, Nnewi.

I immediately left home for the IGS boarding house, where I slept on a mat between the beds of two students; I was a late-comer and the school's dormitories were fully booked. The promotion examinations came up in November 1963 and I was 19th out of thirty-six students. The Principal and my parents were pleasantly surprised by my performance. I moved to Class 5 with my classmates who had also passed the promotion examination. In April 1964, the Class 5 students registered for the Secondary School Leaving Certificate examinations organized by the West African Examinations Council (WAEC). The 1964 school

fees were overdue by May and the students in arrears, including myself, were sent home to collect their fees. It was Imöka Day and Awka
was agog with whip-wielding masquerades followed by expert flute-
blowers (ökwö öja) and a host of ebullient young men. Awka indigenes
do not travel on Imöka Day and the town was in a festive mood. My
mother was absent and the fees would be available the next day. I went
into the Obi and met a raffia masquerade which proposed going to the
Imöka shrine to join the masquerades and men in the mutual whipping (ï-kü agba) show of force. The sound of the irresistible masquerade's flute (öja mmönwü) was all over town. My masquerade rushed
out of the Obi and I followed it, hugging a bunch of whips (anyachü).
We headed for the Ükwüöjï junction to join the mass of masquerades
and young men that had welcomed our Ümüokpu brothers at the
Ngene-ükwa Bridge between Awka and Amawbia. The atmosphere
was charged and the town was rowdy (obodo dü ragaa). As we organized ourselves to move up to the Imöka shrine at Nkwö Amenyi, I noticed one IGS teacher, dressed in white, walking with his bicycle along
the footpath linking the CMS Bookshop to the Ümüenechi-Ükwüöjï
road. The teacher, as a non-indigene, was supposed to stay home as
the Imöka preparation announcements had advised all non-indigenes.
Given the large number of masquerades around, good sense should
have told him to seek refuge in the nearest compound to his right. It
was stupid for him to have kept walking toward a formidable crowd of
masquerades and peped-up young men. Sensing the danger, I rounded
up a few masquerades and men and rushed to protect the unreasonable
teacher. The crowd was dense and before we could reach him a masquerade dancing toward him whipped him on the left shoulder. The
flexible whip struck his shoulder and backside with such a force that
the bicycle fell from his hands. He was on his knees with raised arms
begging the masquerades and men around him for mercy. The same
masquerade that had whipped the teacher surged forward to deliver
another stroke, but my small group grabbed it and formed a protective
shield around the unfortunate teacher. My men picked up his bicycle
cleaned the dirt on his clothes and led him into the side road beside the
present Co-operative Bank, Awka at Ezi Ekweelu. They advised him
to find his way home and avoid contact with masquerades along the
roads. The teacher did not see me, because only initiated persons could
see those who accompanied the masquerades. A few other skirmishes
happened on our way to the shrine. I recall a non-indigene tailor who
was standing at the entrance of his workshop on the ground-floor of

Mr. Akabögü's house at Ezi Ekweelu, opposite the Total petrol station. A masquerade whipped him and he attacked the masquerade. The masquerade bolted away and the tailor went after it. My group went after the tailor and masquerade. The masquerade ran into the bush just before Mr. Adigwe's compound and the tailor followed. That was a big mistake on the part of the tailor. The masquerade stopped and faced the tailor who was advancing angrily towards it to start a fight. My masquerade barked (machaa) and the tailor turned around. Before he realized which way was up, my masquerade's flexible whip hit him hard on his head, the flexible whip striking also his backside. He lurched forward to grip my masquerade and the later simply bent down and raised the tailor in the air like a baby. Before we could restrain my masquerade, it floored the tailor so hard on the ground that the fellow passed out. We left the tailor in the bush, came out to the tarred road and continued our march to the shrine. The sound of the masquerade flutes charged the atmosphere so intensely that a sort of "high" seized both masquerades and men. We felt a sudden invulnerability and leaped over walls without knowing how it happened. We next came across some non-indigene butchers selling meat at Eke Nwïïda, the current Kenneth Dike Park. They were requested to escape immediately before the compact group of men and masquerades arrived. They refused to listen and threatened us with their knives. We surrounded their stalls and some strong men and masquerades mounted on the roofs of the stalls. A light masquerade dance (ï-zö ökïka) on the roofs sent the stalls crashing onto the butchers below. There was stampede and we simply captured all of them. They were thoroughly thrashed and left prostrate with some raw beef in their mouths. Sensing that some non-indigenes were out to create trouble and some unlucky ones could be killed by the irate youth and their masquerades, the organizers of the festival requested that all should trot to the shrine and remain on the tarred road. We did as instructed and passed quickly through Ümüogbunu, Ümüükwa, Ümüdiöka, Ümüzööcha and arrived at the shrine at Nkwö Amenyi. When the mutual whipping (ï-kü agba) show began, the masquerades and their companions exposed their faces in accordance with the rules. Women do not watch this show of endurance and the closest male spectators stood across the tarred road, where Özö Petrol station now stands along the road to Obi Orimili Ndigwe's compound. The companions of masquerades checked themselves out to ensure that none was wearing more than one pair of trousers. Then the bout started. I would put out a leg to receive the whip of some fellow who reciprocates in turn. Men and masquerades filled the Nkwö Amenyi square and traded strokes of the whip. It was getting late and I told my masquerade it was time to go back to the Obi. We covered our faces, crossed the tarred road, and headed home through inter-village shortcuts. We got home in less than forty-five minutes. The masquerade went back to its home in the Obi, while I went into the family house where my fellow human beings dwelt. Being a spirit, the masquerade returned to the spirit world through the Obi altar door (üzö ndi mmöö). It would not accept to come with me because human beings and spirits cannot live together (mmöö na mmadü a-nara e-biko önü). The next morning I got my school fees and went back to school. I later heard that the butchers we had manhandled called in the police and arrested our senior masquerade (nnekwu mmönwü) that had come for the festival's closing ceremony. The arrests took place a few minutes after my masquerade and I crossed the tarred road on our way home.

The school was abuzz with news when I got back. The IGS teacher flogged by a masquerade had reported the matter to the school authorities and a search was underway to find the culprit. The Principal sent word around to find out whether some IGS students participated in the festival. Some Awka students, whistle blowers, who were at the shrine during the mutual whipping show testified they recognized my face in the crowd. Unknown to me and my friends at the mutual whipping arena, the IGS games master, Mr. Akpadiok, had taken photos of the unveiled masquerades and their companions during the mutual whipping show. My face appeared clearly on one of his photos and he presented it to the Principal as the ultimate evidence of my culpability. The Principal summoned me to his office, showed me the photo and asked why I had whipped an IGS teacher. I gave him the whole story, stressing how I had saved the man from probable death at the hands of irate men and masquerades. He asked me to go and check my conscience properly and see him the next day. I saw him the next day and he said: "Please tell me the whole truth. Did you whip the teacher?" I repeated my story of the previous day and added: "I had no reason to whip this man. I have had no contact with him since he lectured Classes 1-3, and I was in Class 5." He seemed convinced but added that my case would be difficult to defend at the school Board in the light of my history at OMGS, Nnewi. He said that my Christian godfather, Mr. B. Umerah, the all-powerful Chairman of the IGS Board and a staunch opponent of heathen festivals, would not even listen to my defense. In spite of my innocence, I would still be expelled from school for attending a pagan festival. The sanction fell on my head two days later: I was summoned to the dinning hall and summarily dismissed in front of the whole school. Since I had registered for the WAEC test, I would come from my home to take the exams. Before he said the closing prayers, I walked out on everybody. I gathered my stuff at nightfall and walked home. My mother was downcast. She went to see Mr. Umerah, the all-powerful IGS Board Chairman. She said that this friend of the family and my godfather had thoroughly humiliated her in the presence of his wife that she had no legs to leave his house (a-fürö m ökpa m ji-füta na be ya). I later went to Mr. Umerah's house and he told me that the masquerade that whipped the teacher had been identified by the organizers of the festival, but that my expulsion was being upheld for my participation—a Christian child and his godson—in an abominable heathen festival. He said all this in the presence of his wife. I was outraged that in spite of my recognized innocence, this Christian bigot wanted to punish me so as to deter Awka youngsters from celebrating the culture of their ancestors. I looked him in the eyes and gave him a good piece of my mind. I told him he could go hang and that Imöka would kill him if he does not stop his bigotry. He was gasping but the look on my face scared his wife who asked him to take it easy and hear me out. I told him that I will come from home to take and pass my WAEC papers to show him that Imöka cannot accept the unwarranted disgrace of Its children. I told him to forget his godfather crap and look at his hypocrite face in a good mirror. I reminded him of how he had mistreated me in 1956 at Government School, Awka, where he was the Headmaster. I was in Standard 5 and ten years old. We had ended a meeting of teachers and students. He asked us to close our eyes for prayers and had said a few words when I screamed because a bully, Lawrence Anekwe, had hit me hard with a whip. I was standing in the back row beside Lawrence, who was twice my age and for which we made fun of him. The Headmaster stopped praying and ordered whoever had screamed to come forward. I moved forward holding the whip and told him that I had screamed because the bully flogged me with the whip. He asked me to give him the whip. He then grabbed my hand, took the whip from me and gave me not less than twelve lashes all over my body. He thundered that I had no business disrupting his prayer session with my stupid scream. The teachers and students were scandalized by what happened. I wailed loudly, rained insults on him, opened my ten fingers towards him and said "waka". In 1956,

Mr. Umerah whipped an eleven-year old mercilessly for disturbing his Christian prayer session, just to prove to the students that his mummery could not be disturbed without the sky coming down on the head of the impertinent culprit. He had to show an example, even with an innocent person. History repeated itself eight years later in 1964 when the same boy, then aged nineteen, was unjustly expelled from secondary school by the same all-powerful Mr. Umerah, Chairman of the IGS Board of Directors. Mr. Umerah had again punished an innocent youngster as an example to show others that participation in pagan rituals was an unforgivable sin against the Holy Ghost. He was startled by my recollection of my encounter with him in 1956 and was unable to hold my gaze. I was bitter against this godfather of mine and stood up to go. His wife was dumbfounded by what she heard, particularly my ability to recall minute details. Her husband tried to offer further explanations, but I gave them one cool look and left. The WAEC papers came up in mid October 1964. My father's body died on October 26, 1964. The WAEC results came out in 1965 and I bagged a Grade 3 pass, to the amazement and befuddlement of my detractors.

With my father gone I was thrown back onto myself. I entered the Civil Service in 1965 after bribing a group of civil servants headed by my uncle, Jerry Ajaana Nnajide, who was a Senior Lands Officer at the Ministry of Lands and Survey, Enugu. Prominent among this group of white-colar criminals was one Mr. Chukwuraa, whose Awka residence is next to Maazï Igweze's (Nwokoye Nweeji's) blacksmith workshop (ünö üzü), going from Dike Park towards St. Faith's Church. He was the group's cashier. We had taken some entrance test, supervised by Uncle Jerry and his group. I waited in vain for the result. Then I approached my sister, Mrs. Joy N. Nwkoye, who sent me to Mr. Chukwuraa to find out what was going on. The man told me that I had been recruited because my result was good. But he added that a fee of two pounds must be paid before I could get my engagement letter. I had no money but I desperately needed a job. I proposed to pay the sum immediately after my first pay and he agreed. I told Uncle Jerry about this bribe thing and he said it was the rule. I got the job and paid the bribe after my first pay. I worked at the Land Office opposite Kingsway Stores Enugu. I later joined the Biafran Army at Enugu in July 1967. We camped and trained at the Enugu prisons. The daily footing itinerary was: Ogbete-Coal Camp-Uwani-Ogui-Ogbete. We later joined Colonel Ifensö's 12th Infantry Batalion at Mfuma, along the Abakaliki-Ogoja road. When part of this Batalion left for the Midwestern Nigeria campaign, Captain

Aneke took charge of my Company, which stayed behind at Mfuma. The Mfuma Bridge was destroyed by the Biafran Army, with a view to preventing a surprise Nigerian offensive from the Ogoja axis. From Mfuma, Capt. Aneke sent me to Umuahia for an interview to attend the School of Infantry at Ihite, Okigwe. The interview panel sent me to IGS Awka to collect my WAEC transcript from the school. My principal, Mr. Ekwoanya, was shaken when he saw me in army uniform. His turbulent student had become a fear-inspiring soldier. I had no weapon but my features were intimidating. He was visibly scared. I saw his problem and calmly assured him that I had forgiven everybody for what happened in 1964. I had come for my transcript, which was required for my entry into the Biafran School of Infantry. His face relaxed and he asked me to come the next day for the transcript. At the Ihite Okigwe School of Infantry, I had a samall group of ebullient friends who had also come to the school from the battle front. We were bored because we saw the school as a place to train intellectual and cultured soldiers. The battle was ragging out there and here are soldiers strutting around and talking grammar. I wondered how officers from this school could lead other soldiers into battle. We broke all the school's rules and the authorities decided not to commission us. Unfortunately for them, mercenary Major Rolf Steiner of the Biafran Commando Unit came looking for volunteer cadets for the formation of his new Commando Division. All the cadets were assembled at a parade and Major Steiner's interpreter explained the implications of being a commando: high death rate and a slim chance of coming out of the war alive, the special training, the special dangerous operations with small units, etc. At the end of his explanations he asked fifty volunteers to step out of the ranks. All members of my gang of ebullient cadets stepped out. Major Steiner inspected us one after the other and selected the ones he wanted. The inspection consisted in standing in front of a volunteer and looking at the pit at the base of the throat just above the breastbone. He read the person's pulse in this way. Colonel Adeleke, the School Commander, commissioned us the next day and we left Ihite Okigwe for the Ihite Orlu Madona High School Commando headquarters. After intensive training at the Madona Camp, I was deployed to the 12th Commando Batalion at Afikpo. The Batalion was commanded by Major Steve, a white mercenary. He was a quiet, ruthless and tenacious soldier. The rest of my army career is history and I hope to pen something about it someday. Let's go on with what is linked directly to Ödïnanï.

My senior brother, Emeke, was studying in Britain and the family had no adult male to sit in for my dead father. I was not bothered about Ödïnanï since uncle Afulukwe was in control. But the situation changed rapidly after the Biafra war. We shall now recount the efforts made since the end of the war to recover and revive Ödïnanï in my family.

THE RECOVERY AND REVIVAL OF ÖDÏNANÏ

We shall now describe the recovery and revival of Ödïnanï in my family. It started with the reconstruction and consecration of the family Obi that knelt down but did not fall during the Biafra war. I was in the Biafran army and the Nigerian soldiers who took Awka went round to identify and destroy the homes of Biafran soldiers. They bombed my family's brick house and the Obi, but spared my grandfather's mud house. This house was roofed with corrugated sheets and had a ceiling, the floor of which was made of white-ant-resistant planks from the trunk of the ubili palm tree. Access into the ceiling was achieved with a movable ladder through a secret manhole on the surface of the ceiling. My great-grandfather's Ödïnanï relics were stored in this ceiling and survived the war: his özö staff (ngwu-agïlïga), oche ajaghïja (ajaghïja title holder's chair), a brass sword, battle shields (ekpeke) and a lot more. All the walls of the Obi collapsed except the one bearing the Iru mmöö (the holy of holies). In accordance with my father's pledge to ensure the physical integrity of the Obi and family Gods, my senior brother, Emeke, rebuilt the Obi. Dibïa Afa guided us during the restoration process and helped us prepare the ritual objects—Öfö, Ikenga, Okpenshi, etc. As mentioned earlier, the Obi is located in my compound but belongs to seven families—the direct descendants of Udoh Anaagö, my great-grandfather. After the Obi came the family Deities—Agwü, Ngwu, Okuku, Akwali Ömümü. My Ümünna were involved—they made symbolic contributions, but I happily bore the brunt of the financing.

Something remarkable happened after the restoration and consecration of the Obi. My uncle, Jerry Ajaana Nnajide, the then Sole Administrator of Onitsha, had problems with Navy Captain Madueke, the Governor of Anambra State. Jerry was arrested and detained. His assets were confiscated and his retirement benefits were cancelled. He pulled all the available human and spiritual strings to no avail. Then we met at the Obi during a family meeting, where his plight was one of the items on the agenda. He had been to the end of the world in search of some God to pull him out of the lion's mouth, but found none. A cousin of mine and a good friend of Jerry took the floor and said: Ndï be anyï, a-shï na ö-nyïzïa Igbo, Awüsa a-gwöba. My people, it is said that we resort to the Hausa Dibïa when the Igbo ones have failed. Ikwu nne m dü Igala. Unu ma na ife-okike dolu fa anya. My mother is Igala and we all know how good they are in the art of "tying" or how spiritually powerful the Igala are. Anyï na-akwakü i-je ikwu nne m, ka e-jee fü ishi okwua. We are preparing to travel to Igala to solve this problem for good. I took the floor and asked Jerry for his permission to plead his case before our ancestors in the Obi. I said: "without prejudice to your trip to Igala, permit me to offer our ancestors kola nuts and a bottle of whiskey immediately, with the promise of a ram, if your dignity is restored quickly." He agreed and I repeated my prayer in front of the Obi altar, with the kola nuts and a bottle of whiskey in my hands. The officiating priest broke the kola nuts, offered a piece to the ancestors and we ate the remainder. The whiskey made the round of the Obi, while the meeting continued. The trip to Igala was scheduled to take place twenty-eight days after our meeting and I went back to Abidjan. Two weeks later, I called my folks at Awka to see how they were doing and they were jubilating. Uncle Jerry was free, his assets were restored to him and his pension benefits were reinstated. The Anambra State government published the good news in its gazette. Thereafter, Governor Mmadueke was removed from office. The trip to Igala was cancelled. Did Uncle Jerry show any appreciation to our ancestors and the Obi? No. He had become a strong member of the Father Ede craze and would have nothing to do again with Dibïa or Ödïnanï. When I came home with my family on vacation, I reminded my folks of my promise to Ndï Ichie when Uncle Jerry was in the lion's mouth. The ritual was fixed to take place seven days hence. My cousin who was to take Jerry to Igala was sent to inform him about the ritual. Jerry failed to show up or justify his absence on the appointed day. We went ahead without him. There was a ram with powerful coiled horns, yams, kola nuts, plenty of palm wine, etc. I told the ancestors that I was fulfilling the promise I made to them regarding Uncle Jerry, when he was in the lion's mouth. I thanked them and requested their understanding for his absence at the ongoing ritual. We had our feast and all went home singing (na-adü ugoli). Uncle Jerry's attitude did not bother me. I, not Uncle Jerry, made the request and promise to Ndï Ichie. Ndï Ichie have done what I requested of them and I have fulfilled the promise tied to my request. Öya naa ofeke, o-chezoo ögwü. Upon recovery from an ailment, the undiscerning forgets his medication. Ö-dï na-njö, a-chöba Dibïa. When really cornered, we look for the Dibïa. A promise to Ndï Ichie is a debt to be cleared as soon as we have the resources to do so. Why? Because, who knows: the frog may trip, fall and break its belly. A-nara amaama ükwü a-kpöö nwa awö ö-daa tibee afö.

We have already spoken at length about the Eucharist rituals and we shall not dwell on them again. We shall focus on the post-war reconstitution of some outmoded rituals. Revival of Ödïnanï should be high on the agenda of the enlightened Igbo. By the enlightened Igbo I mean those that have seen through the lie of Christianity concerning Ödïnanï. Christianity has done and continues to do untold damage to the mind of Igbo children by the intense desecration and disparagement of Ödïnanï. The family, the Christian priest and the school stuff the mind of youth with lies about a God the liars know nothing about. The Igbo youth can hardly think for themselves—the Christian priest and the Bible do all the thinking for them. I had around me a few young Bible pundits who have made at least five unsuccessful attempts at the JAMB[5] hurdle; they wasted useful time and energy at Bible classes, all-night-vigils, prayer warrior sessions and church work carefully elaborated by the scheming priests. The church harvest envelopes reached the extended family through these slaves of priest-craft.

Revival of Ödïnanï in my entourage combines mental housecleaning with ritual. On weekends a few young as well as elderly folks gather at my family Obi and we chat about philosophy and religion. There is toddy palm wine (nkwü), raffia palm wine (ngwö) and the usual Obi hot drink (njenje, kaï-kaï, akpürü achïaa). Since our young pundits read the Bible with closed eyes I have placed a KJV Bible in a corner of the Obi, just in case we have to re-read some portions together with open eyes. A philosophical or religious question is raised by a member of the group. Members propose answers and explanations. The young and old give their views. The best-fit answer or explanation normally gets majority approval. One such question was the difference between Ndï üka (Christians) and Ndï ö-gö mmöö (followers of Ödïnanï). I told the audience that we are all Ndï ö-gö mmöö since Chineke is Mmöö. The only difference is in etu (ele) e-si (e-shi) a-gö nyabü mmöö, the ritual. Chineke or Mmöö is one, but the ways of communing with It are many and equivalent. Ödïnanï is the Igbo way that suffices unto

---

5 Joint Admissions and Matriculation Board conducts Matriculation Examination for entry into all Universities, Polytechnics and Colleges of Education (by whatever name called) in Nigeria.

itself. Seeing the positive impact of my explanation on the young ones, I invited them the next Sunday to my periodic Eucharist with Ndï Ichie in the family Obi. There was plenty to eat and drink, and every step in the ritual was explained for the benefit of the youngsters.

Chi, reincarnation, sex, sin, the devil, and ï-gba agü (the ritual to determine who has reincarnated in a child) are some of the regular topics of discussion. The best part of the revival effort is that once the youth have thrown the mental thrash of mind-warping religious indoctrination, they never go back to the foolishness of wasting their good time on meaningless religious mummery. They spend their time usefully in creative play, work or rest. They read and cultivate the mind above all. They now read the Bible with open eyes and query its contents, if they don't understand. They discover that true prayer has everything to do with their personal Chi in their bodies and nothing to do with the Christian Jesus or some God in the high heavens. They take their lives into their hands instead of depending on unscrupulous and scheming Christian priests.

Ödïnanï has been a men's affair. This segregation pushed our women and young male children into the hands of Christianity. The Ödïnanï ritual fixed on an Eke Sunday shows the lady of the house leaving for the church with the little ones, since there will be nobody to look after them in her absence when the ritual moves into gear. By the time the boys reach the age of taking active part in the rituals, we discover that the Christian virus has taken root in them. To such children Ödïnanï is simply crass superstition, idol or devil worship.

The role of women in Ödïnanï is under study, with a view to bringing them back into the fold of Igbo religion. In this connection, we have had Afa sessions with Dibïa Afa in the family Obi. For the issue of women cooking for the Ödïnanï rituals, we had two pieces of paper for i-ji ogu. On one piece we wrote "women can cook for Ödïnanï rituals" and on the other piece we wrote "women cannot cook for Ödïnanï rituals". The two pieces of paper were rolled into balls, taken outside the Obi, and bound to speak the truth by spraying aja ana (sand) on them. Thus blessed, the two balls of paper were dropped on the Obi floor in front of the seated Dibïa Afa. He took the paper balls in turn and eventually presented us with one of them asking us to follow whatever is written on it: unu ga-eso ogu nkea. We unfolded the paper ball which read "women cannot cook for Ödïnanï rituals." Next we asked: Can the women serve anything during the Ödïnanï rituals? The answer was again negative. Finally, we asked, almost in despair: Can women eat the Ödïnanï meals—azü amalu-ile (blessed smoked catfish with pepper, salt and palm oil), kola nut, wine, food? The answer was YES! The new dispensation is: The men cook and serve during the Ödïnanï rituals. The women are invited to come and celebrate with their husbands, brothers and sons.

My grand-uncle's wife, Nwanyanwü Nweke (Özala) from Ümüzööcha village, Awka, had her Chi altar comprising a water-filled terra cotta plate (ökü) placed at the base of an ögbü tree (ögbü na-enye ndo!). She venerated her Chi every year and always asked me, in the absence of elders, to break the kola nut and kill the cock for her. I was in primary school then. For the feast, she offered us roasted yam and chicken. She told me that the Chi is her sole guardian when, because of marriage, she left her maiden home. N'ije di, ö bü sö mü na Chi m yï-eje. This powerful lady helped me trace my origins. She gave me an elaborate family tree that included women—a rare feat, since only the men count in our genealogy.

On the village and town levels the various Alüshï are getting moral and material support.

I tell my folks that Ödïnanï is eternal. Greed and ignorance have pushed our dumskull brethren into the abomination of destroying the symbols of Ödïnanï with the help of scheming Christian priests. Well, the temerarious fools destroy the symbols but not the indestructible thing symbolized—Spirit. The visitation of Ödïnanï on these fellows has been immediate and dolorous. Some go nuts and wander through life zombie-like, na-eje e-fuo m e-fuo m. Some lose their lives. The repentant ones replace the destroyed objects and do the necessary purification rites. I know of no family that ever had peace after destroying Ödïnanï symbols with the help of Christian priests. And what is the retribution for the marauding priests? Practically none, since they are guests invited by our people. The Christian priests know their trade and always act on engineered invitation. Some of my folks have ears, not for hearing, but as decorative outgrowths. Their bodies hear better than their ears, arü fa ka ntï fa a-nü ife. And they learn the hard way.

I repeat: We can see the symbol of a spirit, not the spirit itself. The tortoise is an apt symbol of the Awka God Imöka. But the tortoise is not the God Itself. The God is breath, spirit or wind, and cannot be seen! But this breath can momentarily take hold of and use the body of a man, python or tortoise. It is then the unseen mover of the man, python or tortoise.

I have advised my friends who want to remove the symbols of

Ödïnanï left behind by their ancestors to employ the servic
Dibïa Afa and avoid creating clutter with the Christian priests. Using
a Christian priest to destroy Ödïnanï ritual objects assumes that the
priest knows how those objects were made and consecrated. We might
as well disarm a land mine by pouring holy oil and water on it. In
Ödïnanï, the way up is the only way down (ebe e-shi a-lïgo ka e-shi a-
lïtu). To ignore this rule is to court disaster and unnecessary trouble.

My people say: Ö-bïalü be onye a-bïagbunie, ö-naba mkpu afük-
wanïa n'azü. Bring no bad omen to the house of your host, so there will
be no crying and wailing when you depart. E-mebikwana afa gï; maka
na ezigbo afa ka ego. Drag not your name in the mud; because a good
name has greater value than money. It is this profound philosophy that
explains the legendary Igbo sense of hospitality.

Christianity has trampled and continues to trample this Igbo philosophy and sense of hospitality underfoot by attacking our roots in
Ödïnanï. We know that Christianity, as our guest, will go someday.
Since this marauding and undiscerning guest has brought us a bad
omen, there will be plenty of crying and wailing when it departs from
our midst. Misery and death is the lot of those who desecrate Ödïnanï.
Anï says: tifulu m mkpu, mana rafülü m ögü. Speak out in my defence
but leave the fighting for me. So let me ask the Igbo in whose midst the
Christians are attacking Ödïnanï without any justification: I tifugolu
Anï nkpu? Have you spoken out in defence of Anï? He who remains
silent consents. The snake of retribution bites the direct perpetrators
of evil and whips the silent consenters with its tail. Agwö a-taghï ata,
ö-jüö ödüdü.

MORNING PRAYER IN THE OBI—Ï GÖFÜLÜ NDÏ ICHIE ÖJÏ ÜTÜTÜ

The morning kola nut offering ritual may be performed anywhere,
but we shall present its performance in the Obi (temple). The ritual may
be broken down into: self-cleansing with a seed of the alligator pepper,
invocations with a piece of kaolin, invocations with the kola nut, breaking of the kola nut and deciphering the oracle given by the spread of
the kola nut lobes, removing the "tongues" on the lobes (ile öjï) and
throwing them outside for the powers that be, eating of the kola nut
lobes, libation with njenje (Igbo gin). I have been advised to open the
alligator pepper pod behind my back and to avoid spilling the seeds
on the Obi floor. Non-observance of the behind-the-back stuff may give

headache to those who eat the pepper. Walking on spilled pepper seeds may provoke unexplainable quarrels among those in the Obi.

I wash my hands with clean water. Taking one seed of the alligator pepper (ose örö or ose öjï) between the thumb and the next finger, I touch my forehead, mouth, chest and two legs with the fingers holding the seed, repeating öraakwü füö! (negative vibes, get out!) as I do so. I swing the hand holding the seed trice around my head saying anya m a-fükörö ntï m, beelü sö ma m ji enyo (except with a mirror, my eyes cannot see my ears.) I throw the seed out of the Obi. Finally, I chew seven seeds of ose öjï to wake me up fully, because ose öjï a nara-eme anyaüla (the alligator pepper dissipates sleepiness.) This cleansing process with the alligator pepper seed is called ï-chüfü öraakwü, ï-jücha arü (body cleansing).

The invocations now follow. I have provided English equivakents of the invocations. They are not perfect, but they give some idea of the concepts expressed. Following the cleansing is the invocation with a piece of kaolin (ï-tü nzu). The saying of each stanza is followed by the scraping of the kaolin with the thumb and the dropping of the scraped powder on the floor beside you. Ï-tü nzu (Ï-ma nzu) comes from this dropping or throwing (ï-tü) of the kaolin powder (nzu). We thus offer kaolin, white earth, to the powers that be.

(1)   Chi m bïa tüö nzu. (My God come and take kaolin)
(2)   Ife na-emelü anyï ife na ife anyï na-emelü ife bïa-nü tüö nzu. (The powers that work for us and those we work for, come and take kaolin)
(3)   Ife öma meelü anyï mböshï Eke, mböshï Oye, mböshï Afö na mböshï Nkwö. (May good things befall us on Eke day, Oye day, Afö day, and Nkwö day)

I now draw four vertical lines for the four marketdays of the Igbo week and cross (or encircle) them with a fifth line for my Chi. I finally mark my feet, forehead and one eye with the kaolin.

I wash a kola nut with clean water and place it in the wooden kola nut bowl (any flat plate having some depth will do). I hold the bowl comfortably with the right hand. The invocation for breaking the kola nut follows.

(1)   Chukwu, Amaamaamachaamacha, bïa taa öjïa n'otu ka anyï taa nya n'ibe. (God-the-Father-Mother, The Great and unknown, come and eat this kola nut as one piece so that we can eat the pieces)
(2)   Chineke maalü onye ö ga-eke, mana onye ö ga-eke amarïa, biko

bïa taa öjï. (Creator of the universe, God-the-Son, you know your creatures but they know you not; please come and eat kola nut)

(3) Obunaana bïa taa öjï. (God of the Earth and Its hierarchies, come and eat kola nut)

(4) Ndï Mmili, Ndï Ikuku, Ndï Ökü, Anyanwü na Agbala bïak-waa-nü taa öjï. (Spirits of Water, Air, Fire, the Sun and Rainbow, come and eat kola nut)

(5) Chi m bïa taa öjï. (My God, come and eat kola nut)

(6) Imökanoome, Akeeteögba, Mgbaghanyïlïazï, biko bïa taa öjï. (Imöka the just, Akeete the great python, the baffler of the youth, please come and eat kola nut)

(7) Ngeneonyeachönam, Nnenwaanya tinyelu ike na mmïli, bïa taa öjï. (Ngene, the war goddess whose butt dips into the river, come and eat kola nut)

(8) Alüshï niine dï n'Öka bïa taa öjï. (The Gods of Awka, come and eat kola nut)

(9) Ichie Ukwu na Ichie Nta, Ökpü Ukwu na Ökpü Nta, bïa-nü taa öjï. (Dead and living elders, dead and living daughters, come and eat kola nut)

(10) Ndï ö na-abü e-kuo ö-dï mma na ndï ö na-abü e-kuo ö-dï njö, bïa-nü taa öjï. (Ministering and avenging spirits, come and eat kolanut)

(11) Maka na ndï öbüna nwelü ulu fa na-aba. (Because each group of spirits has its utility)

(12) Onye öbüna maküö Chi ya ka Chi anyï wee maküö Chineke bü onye ma`külü Chukwu. (Let each person embrace his God so that the latter will embrace the Creative God, which already embraces the Great Unknown God)

(13) A shï m na nwoke na nwaanya ga-adï ndü, arü e-shie fa ike, uche e-zuo fa oke. (May man and woman live long and be whole in body and mind)

(14) Maka na üwa a-nara atö ütö ma a-dï ndü, nwee arü ike, mana uche e-zuro oke. (Because life loses its savor when we live long and are strong, but the mind is not whole)

(15) A na m ekene maka ife unu meelü anyï, na-ekenekwa maka nke unu ka ga-eme eme. (I give thanks for what you did for us and for what you will do for us)

(16) Nye-nü anyï nwa-oo, na anyï achörö ümü na-amünye ökü n'ünö. (Give us the child, we do not want ruffians that would

torch the house)

(17) A shï m a-müö nwoke nya bülü nwoke; a-müö nwaanya nya bülü nwaanya ka ö-baa ulu nwaanya na-aba. (Let our males be true males and let our females be true females, because females have a special utility)

(18) Njanja ikpu kakwa-nü örü nshï mma; maka na a-maka ikpu ajö njö, nya bü üzö e-shi a-bïa üwa. (The ugliest vagina is better than the anus; for, however ugly the vagina may be, it is the door through which we come into this world)

(19) Wete-nü ife anyï ga-eli, ünü e-wetene nke ga-eli anyï. (Give us what to eat, not what will eat us)

(20) Biko wenete-nü eziokwu na udo, ka ö-dïkwa ka ö-dï gboo mgbe nwaanya na-ala di ya. (Please bring us truth and peace, and restore the old dispensation when the woman made love to her husband)

(21) Maka na ngbe gboo na ö-bü nwaanya na-ala di ya. (Because it was the woman who made love to her husband in the good old days)

(22) Mana ö-bü eri nwoke ji-kete nkwücha ï-la nwaanya ka chi ji wee-jineri odogwu na mgbaachi. (Darkness befell man at midday since he took it upon himself to start making love to the woman)

(23) Ife dï na ngada dolu nwaanya anya, mana ume nwoke atürö ya. (Whereas man is very limited in the science of sex, the woman is a maestro)

(24) Onye shï ka nke anyï mebie, biko bulunu-üzö mebie nke onye-anwu ka ö-fü ka o shi-adü. (Visit evil on those who wish us evil, so they can see what it feels like)

(25) A bü m nwata na-aghü arü n'afö n'afö. (I am a child that bathes only its belly)

(26) M welü aka nwata bunye unu öjï-a, biko welü-nü aka ögalanya wee nalü m nya. (Accept this kolanut with kingly hands, though my hands be those of a child)

(27) Maka na nwaakanrï shï na nya adïrö mkpümkpü, na ö-bü ike gwülü uto. (The dwarf said that he is not short, but that growth got tired)

(28) Anyï ga-adï ka echi maka na echi a-nara agwüagwü. (May we be like the eternal tomorrow)

(29) Ife öma meelü anyï-oo! (May good things befall us!)

(30) Ka m gölü ka o-lelü, maka na önü nwaakanrï bü önü nna ya-oo.

(My words shall come to pass, because the dwarf's voice is the voice of his ancestors)

(31) Iseee! (Amen! Said by the audience only)

The kolanut is now broken and gently thrown into the wooden bowl. The spread of the lobes is a coded message from Ndï Ichie that may be interpreted by those who know the art. The last invocation concerns libation with njenje (Igbo gin). I take about half a tumbler of njenje and say:

(1) Ka m gölü n'öjï, ka m na-agö na mmanyaa. (What I said with the kolanut applies to this drink)

(2) Öfö solu öfö lee. (The realization of my present prayer shall dovetail with that of the previous one)

Then I sprinkle the altar and the ritual objects, leaving a small quantity that I can drink or give to some loved one to drink. This is mmanya a-tülü atü (blessed wine). The libation is poured outside if one is not authorized to do so at the altar. Now we can eat and drink freely after eating and drinking with the Gods and our ancestors. E ligbe, ömïmï a-naa! Ill feelings disappear after an Eucharist feast!

Note that the thirty-one invocation stanzas given above contain three levels. The first level concerns the invitation of the Rulers. The second level relates to a show of appreciation to them and the third level relates to our requests and comments. The content of the levels could be varied at will, depending on the circumstances. When there are visitors, the ritual is short and only key verses are said. When I am alone, for instance, I will normally call my ancestors by name and title. It's lengthy. The same would apply to all the Gods of my family, village and town. I would even include non-indigenous Gods and Goddesses that have been propitious to me or my people. The Goddess Raba of Agulu would have been invoked as: Raba Agülü, Nne mülü ömümü, Ezenwaanya, Onyeöcha bu na mmili, Baabaaduuduu, biko bïakwa taa öjï. There are hair-raising verses that I have not included because their use is dictated by circumstances. In times of diffuculty my morale would be peped-up by the self-encouragement given in the statements:

Mekete mekete a-nara agwü ike (Action tires nobody)

Maka na ö bülü na mekete mekete na-agwü ike (Because, if action was tiring)

Ife omume a ka-akwüshï n'aka nnaa fa (Action would have ended with my ancestors)

Nya bü na a na m eme na nna-nna m melü, nna m mee (So, I am act-ing because my grandfather acted and my father acted too)

Ö gara aghö m ö gara enu m (My actions will not fail and will not be futile)

These invocations are incantations aimed at giving us the spiritual high required for the day's activities. The words invoke images to stir your spirit, giving it a vibratory power that can move mountains. A good invocation may give goose bumps and even bring tears! Thus this "language" is that of incantations or of Mantras, as they are called in India, sound being the most potent and effectual magic agent, and the first of the keys which opens the door of communication between Mortals and the Immortals. It is not surprising that this ritual is the first thing the Igbo man does in the morning. Indeed, no prayer can be more powerful than a well-crafted early morning incantation voiced in your mother tongue. You mentally see what you say and that arouses your God. The resulting magic is natural and guaranteed. We may now understand why reciting prayers from some prayer book or from memory yields no result whatsoever. It is just a recitation of empty words, i.e., words not associated with the corresponding mental images. It's sheer mummery!

Our ancestors knew how to pray with a view to getting results. They worked with Nature and Nature took good care of them. Christianity has endeavored and still endeavors to give us ready-made prayers that are incapable of stirring the human spirit. When a man's source of spiritual power is destroyed, he is mollified and becomes manipulable. I feel really sad when I see people rushing to some Christian gathering to fight for a drop of holy water or oil. The wily Christian priests have taken and are still taking away our time-tested religious practices. They replace them with mind-warping and inefficacious practices that simply bewilder us.

Wake up, Ndï Igbo! The powerful and result-oriented religion of your ancestors, Ödïnanï, is still there and alive. Christianity has just covered it with dust. Remove the dust and let the glory of Ödïnanï shine forth again for our true salvation. The Christian dust is mental and can be thrown anytime we realize that we have been fooled.

Ebunu shï shi-gbaalü ya afa ndü, shi a-gbanalü ya afa ude, maka na onye dï ndü ga-ede ude. The ram asked the oracle for information on its future health and not on its future fame, because whoever is healthy will become famous. The Igbo never prayed for fame. They prayed for life because of their belief that whoever is alive shall become famous. We are all here for some purpose and all we need is a healthy body and mind to excel in our various pursuits. The Igbo mindset would be ordered thus: have a healthy body and mind, work hard in your field, and reap the fame that accrues from your hard-work and expertise in your field. In this connection: Nkïta shï shi-tüfülü ya ökpükpü, ma shi-rafülü ya ife nya na ndï mmöö ga-eje. The dog says: throw the bone to me and don't bother about how I will share it with the spirits.

ÖDÏNANÏ AND SEX

The Igbo was a natural person until Christianity arrived with its mind-warping dogmas. Women were scantily dressed: the married woman had one piece of wrapper tied above the breasts; the wrapper is secured further by a cloth-rope (mgbado) tied around the waist. Her underwear was a miniskirt (ögödü imeukwu) made of a heavy dark-blue cotton cloth (agbö). The unmarried woman left her breasts open and covered her genitals with a few rolls of beads (jigida) around the waist. The young man had a loincloth covering the genitals in front and most of the butt at the back. The tying of this cloth was an art. When properly tied, it was impossible to rip it off the wearer by simply pulling at it. During the full moons, boys and girls play (egwuönwa) together at the village square. They sing, dance, and do hide-and-seek (nzuzo). The seeker is blindfolded by someone who chants: nzuzo nzuzo-oo, o-zolu ka o-zolu zoshikwee ike, agü na-arakwaa m nya (hidding, oh hidding, the hidden should hide very well, because I am letting go the leopard). Meanwhile the playmates disperse to hide in nooks and corners around the square. The blindfold is now removed and the seeker goes in search of the hidden playmates. The girls took pleasure in pulling at the boys' loincloths to see which ones would come off. He whose loincloth comes off attracted ridicule and oppro-brium; his name would figure in the moonlight songs of mockery. The youth played together and were used to their bodies. There was no lust because the joys of sexual intercourse were the privilege of mar-ried couples. The boys were thus groomed to bide their time until they reached adulthood at around twenty-two years of age. The girls un-derwent training on how to woo their husbands, take care of the home and raise children.

Adultery occurred only when a married woman got pregnant for a non-member of her husband's clan. A married woman getting pregnant for a member of her husband's clan is considered a blessing because the bloodline is the same. In such cases no one makes trouble because ishi mkpi ka-dï n'akpa mkpi, the he-goat's head is still in the he-goat's bag. Most of such cases arise when, for professional reasons, husbands leave their wives at home for long periods. It is customary for some clansmen to remain behind in the village to take care of the families of the absent clansmen. They guard the clan and their duty is called i-chedo ünö (watching over the clan). This is why the woman married into the clan is called nwunye-anyï, our wife. Divorce occurred only when the married woman violates some rule that is sacred to the clan. Some examples are: grabbing, pulling and squeezing her husband's testicles; getting pregnant for a non-clansman; desecrating the clan's sacred objects and shrines. The divorce is never total because there are rituals for apology and reconciliation. Marriages in Awka may break but they never come to an end. (Di Öka a-nara ebu-ebu)

Nudity was natural to my ancestors until the repressed and vicious missionaries showed up in our midst. Recall how my grandmother became one of the pioneer Christian converts and the first woman to wear a blouse in Awka. To these missionaries, she was naked and irresistibly alluring. They had to cover her beautiful body before her magnetism pulls out their repressed sexuality. Poor repressed missionaries, they would burst asunder with all the exquisite nudity surrounding them. Their repressed sexuality surfaced with full force and they were going nuts. Just imagine a bunch of Christian priapic priests doing their indoctrination job with a permanently erect penis. They had to cover the source of the distraction. Free clothing was distributed to our womenfolk! And Great Priapus went underground, biding Its time.

The subject of sex was taboo in my family. My mother, who was in charge of our education, did not tolerate any discussions concerning sex. A Christian child must avoid such babblings (i-kwu ofega, ï-kö önü efu). It was sin and punishable by God. While in secondary school, I once invited a girl to my room. My mother had gone to the market. The girl, on her way in, had greeted my father who was sitting under a tree. He seemed not to be bothered about the girl's visit. So, I bolted my door and relaxed beside my visitor. We reviewed my pile of photo albums and listened to music. Our strategy was that my visitor would leave before my mother came back from the market. But time passed so quickly that none of us realized it was already late afternoon. We suddenly heard my mother talking to my father in the outer court. The girl was frightened but I reassured her. I told her that there should be no problem, since my father was aware of her presence and we had done nothing wrong. My mother went to her room, which was next to mine. Hearing the music and conversation coming from my room, she tried to enter my room through the door that linked our rooms. But the door was bolted from my end. She left her room, went into the parlor and came to the door that linked my room to the veranda. Finding this door also bolted, she banged repeatedly on it shouting: Ïmaniel, kpöghee uzo-nünwa ösö-ösö! (Emmanuel, open this door immediately!). I had anticipated her move and had my hand on the bolt when she started banging on the door. I opened the door wide enough for her to see the girl. I then closed the door behind me and walked towards my mother. She was startled by my behavior and stepped backwards. Seeing that she was probably scared, I stopped walking towards her and asked her why she was so upset by the presence of a girl in my room. She said it was a sin for unmarried men and women to lock themselves up in a room. She was hysterical, saying that the girl must leave immediately. I agreed and asked her to relax while I went into my room to ask the girl to leave. When the girl and I emerged from my room, my mother was waiting for us. She gave the girl some verbal lashing and forbade her to visit me again. She wanted to know who her parents were, in order to go and warn them about her visits to my home. The humiliation was too much for me and I dragged the girl away before she had time to give her identity to my enraged mother. I escorted the girl out of the compound and both of us sat under a tree to cool off a bit. When I came back to the house, my mother called me and wanted to talk about the issue. Without saying a word, I simply rose from my seat and walked to my room ignoring her orders to come back for her sermon. After this incident, I decided to meet my girlfriends everywhere except in my home.

Whatever I know about man-woman relationship came from friends. Key among these friends are Fabian Okeke, Emma Obierika and his cousin David Enemchukwu, the kind boxing champ at OMGS Nnewi. They are all from Nnewi. It was in 1961. I was in Class 2, Emma and Fabian were in Class 3, and David was in Class 4. The school was on a two-week midterm vacation. Most of the students had gone away and the four of us were among the few who stayed on campus. Emma, David and I were in House A (Ojukwu House, later). Emma and I were friends. He grew up in Lagos and was broadminded. It was a Saturday. Fabian had visited Emma and they were looking at some photos of girls Emma had met during the last long vacation. Emma invited me to join them. I asked him to explain how he managed to have such an array of beautiful girlfriends. He said he talked to them and struck up a tie of friendship, which he kept alive with letters. If a girl caught his fancy, he would walk up to her and strike some conversation (tune her up!) and follow-up with further meetings. I was speechless. He asked me about my girlfriends and I said I had none. He laughed and promised to fix something for me. He promised to ask David to lecture us the following day on the subject of stopping a girl and talking to her. We had breakfast on Sunday morning and assembled at David's cubicle, whose window faced the tarred Nnewi-Owerri road. David sat at his study table, while Emma, Fabian and I sat on his wooden bed facing the window. Our dormitory windows were hinged onto the top of the window frames and wooden poles were used to push the windows outwards, away from the base of the frame. The shortest pole allowed you to open a window in such a way as to see people outside without being easily seen. David started with the most difficult part: making contact with the girl and engaging in some dialogue.

His first recommendation was to be natural in all situations. This is a game that you may win or loose. If you win, it's fine. If you lose, just thank the girl for having given you attention and move on till some other time. The opening sentences would go like this:

Excuse me for disturbing you. Your face looks familiar. Are you not from my hometown, Awka? My name is Emma.

Now wait for her raction. If you interest her, she will open a dialogue with you and introduce herself, eventually. Get her co-odinates and fix a rendezvous to continue the discussion. If she shows up at the rendezvous, propose friendship to her. Flow with events and don't push too much. In case of resistance on the part of a girl, ask for an appointment to give her time to think about your proposal.

I asked David about when to talk to a girl about sex. He explained that it came naturally with the development of the friendship between a boy and a girl. He said: start with friendship, the girl will propose sex when the time comes. To reach the top of a hill, we must first get to its foot. Mgbe ndï be-anyï ji wee-lüba ugwu Ömüko aka, fa a-lïkpügo ya. When our folks start pointing at the Ömüko hill, they will surely get to its summit. The lecture was brief and straight to the point. While we talked David looked out of his window and saw a girl standing under a Melina tree close to the school gate. He asked for a volunteer to try out his lecture on this girl. We looked out, saw the girl and sat down looking sheepishly at each other. David said: So I have just wasted my time lecturing a bunch of cowardly kids on how to become men. I stood up and told them I was going out there to bring the girl with me. I walked up to the girl and said:

Good morning. The school is on midterm break. Have you come to visit some relative of yours? My name is Emma.

She thanked me for being so kind and a dialogue ensued. She lived at Onitsha and her brother was a fellow student at OMGS, etc., etc. I asked her to come and have a soft drink before catching a bus back to Onitsha. She accepted. As both of us turned from the tarred road and walked back to the dormitory, I noticed my friends ducking away from the window. The cubicle was clean and empty by the time I got there with the girl. I made her comfortable, explained that the cubicle belonged to a friend that I would introduce shortly. David, Emma and Fabian came in and I introduced them as my friends. She also introduced herself and I left to get some soft drink and snacks across the tarred road. I entertained her, took her co-ordinates and accompanied her to catch a bus back to Onitsha. My friends were enchanted and proud of me. David was particularly happy that his crisp lecture had worked its magic with such promptitude. I was simply elated! Emma, Fabian and I formed a formidable team of Don Juans. Sex was not the issue. David's lesson worked like magic: if the girl proposes sex, fine; if she doesn't, relax and flow with events. The bliss came from having a retinue of girlfriends, who enjoyed my company. We had a common hobby: music and dancing. My outings with Emma and Fabian took us to the hottest night spots of Onitsha, particularly Dolphin Café Hotel with Rex Lawson and Central Hotel with Celestine Ükwü.

It was at Central Hotel that I met a woman who gave exquisite and requisite sexual instruction to me and my friends. We had gone to Onitsha on a Friday evening and stayed at Fabian's place. Around nine in the evening, we set off to Central Hotel hoping to get a free ticket to the dance hall. I was a champion twist (egwu-ökü) dancer! We were hanging out in front of the hotel when a lady called out to us from a window on the first floor of the hotel. We looked up but it was not clear who she was calling on. Emma pointed at himself, but the lady shook her head sideways. He pointed at Fabian and she did the same thing. I looked elsewhere thinking it was a joke, but Emma shook me and pointed at the lady. She was bekoning me to come to the gate where the guards were screening those going into the hotel. When I got to the gate, she was beside the guards who ushered me in. I gave her room number to my friends from the window through which she had called me. She lived alone and the photo of a boy who looked like me adorned her bedside table. I took a good look at this beautiful, fascinating and fairskinned woman. She said: You and your friends must be students looking for fun in town. Have you had something to eat yet? Let me give some food and drinks to you and your friends and then we can talk. I told her to consult my friends outside and to give me just a small bottle of stout. She soon came back with the small stout for me and a bottle of star beer for herself. She sat on the bed while I took the chair close to the bed. She looked into my face and both of us smiled, like old acquaintances. Pointing at the photo on her bedside table she said: That's my junior brother and you look just like him. She was training the boy in secondary school but no member of her family knew where she lived and what profession she exercised. She was intrigued to see someone like him around her place of work. She thought maybe the boy had located her and had come to see her. We laughed and embraced each other. She gently grabbed my genitals during the emabrace and moved away towards her wardrobe. She undressed and asked me if I liked her body. It was a stunning sight. She helped me to undress. I was on fire. She showed me a pair of dark spots under her arms close to the armpit, which helped her to detect clients with sexually transmissible diseases. She receives an electric shock whenever she touches the genitals of a carrier of disease. She had checked me out during our embrace. She taught me foreplay and restraint to avoid premature ejaculation. I then lay on my back and she made love to me. She was seated on me. We held hands and I just had to squeeze her hands to signal any impending orgasm, so that she could stop all movement and enable me to calm down. I got lessons on sexual hygiene and a licence to visit her on any Sunday that I chose. I could come in the morning and go back to school with a night bus. She forbade me to hang out with schoolgirls or any other woman in the hotel. She said school girls know nothing about sex hygiene and could get pregnant for me. She said: Come here anytime you feel like and just face your studies. It was almost daybreak when she let me go. She came to the window to apologize to my friends and asked us to come together on any Sunday morning. We did, and she gave us mind-blowing lessons on the art of sex. And she never took money from any of us. This woman was a Prostitute to the world around her, but she was a Goddess of love and wisdom to me and my friends. It was after meeting her that the meaning of the words of my farm companion at Ajali downed on me. Recall that the nymph had asked me to urinate inside her vagina. This idea of urinating in her vagina intrigued me and I thought I would try it someday when I grew up and became stronger. But the urination and the urine in question all came naturally after puberty. I was just four years old when a woman (a girl) took me to the door of the temple of the sex Goddess. Twelve years later, the Goddess herself came to the temple door and took me to her Adytum and finished off my initiation.

The colonialist came to the Igbo with his technology and his Christian religion. We should have accepted his technology and politely rejected his ineffectual and mind-warping religion, as did the Chinese and the Japanese. We did not, and this was the Igbo "loss of nerve".

Colonialism is a crusade for political power and the colonization strategy is:

(1) Use military might to subjugate foreign lands and their peoples.

(2) Use mind-warping religious doctrines to mollify the conquered peoples and render them docile.

Fear has been used as a potent weapon to mollify man and render him docile. Once a man is full of fear he loses trust in himself and he is ready to submit. Then he is ready to believe in any stupidity. You cannot make a man believe in nonsense if he has self-trust.

The above facts explain the observed governance tandem involving the politician and the priest. The priest produces the mollified and docile man, which the politician uses for the achievement of his selfish objectives. And that is how man has been exploited down the ages. This is the very trade secret of the so-called religions: make man afraid, make man feel unworthy, make man feel guilty, make man feel that he is just on the verge of hell.

How to make man so afraid? The only way is: condemn life, condemn whatsoever is natural. Condemn sex because it is the fundamental of life; condemn food because that is the second fundamental of life; condemn relationship, family, friendship, because that is the third fundamental of life. We find the following in the Christian Bible's Gospel according to Matthew:

Mat 10:37 He that loveth father or mother more than me is not worthy of me: and he that loveth son or daughter more than me is not worthy of me.

Mat 19:29 And every one that hath forsaken houses, or brethren, or sisters, or father, or mother, or wife, or children, or lands, for my name's sake, shall receive an hundredfold, and shall inherit everlasting life.

The above verses are some of the mind-boggling words put into the mouth of Jesus by the scheming priests who compiled the Christian Bible. Whatsoever is natural to man, condemn it and say it is wrong: "If you do it, you will suffer for it. If you don't do it, you will be rewarded. Hell is going to descend on you if you go on living naturally and heaven will be given to you if you go against life." That is the message of the so-called religions, particularly Christianity.

This means that God will accept you only if you are suicidal. If you slowly commit suicide in the senses, in the body, in the mind, in the heart, and you go on destroying yourself, the more you succeed in destroying yourself, the more you will become beloved to God. This has been the whole teaching of the religions. This has contaminated, poisoned and warped the mind of man.

And the greatest way to create fear is to make man feel guilty about natural things. He cannot drop them, and he cannot enjoy them because of the fear of hell, so he is in a double bind. That double bind is the basis of man's exploitation. We cannot just drop our sexuality because some stupid priest is saying that it is wrong. It has nothing to do with our idea of right and wrong; it is something natural, something in our very being. It is the wind of the spirit blowing wherever it wills. We have come out of it. Since saying is not doing (o-kwukwu a-bürö o-mume!) we cannot drop sex just by saying. But we can start repressing it, and by repressing we go on accumulating it in the unconscious part of the mind, and that becomes a wound. And the more we repress, the more obsessed we become with it. And the more obsessed we become, the guiltier we feel. It is a vicious circle. Now we are caught in the trap of the priest.

And the priest himself has never believed in it, neither has the politician ever believed in it. These things were for the people, the masses, the idiotai, the rabble; the masses have been fooled. The stories say that kings used to have hundreds of wives, and so was the case with priests. And it is a miracle that people continue to believe in these charlatans.

There is an old saying, "Fool me once, shame on you. Fool me twice, shame on me." But the priests have been fooling us down the ages, and they have fooled us so long that it is now almost an accepted phenomenon. It has been so ancient that we take it for granted; nobody thinks that they are being fooled.

The priest goes on inventing more and more tortures for us. He has not allowed us to enjoy anything. Dance is wrong because it is bodily. Laughter is wrong because it depicts weakness of character. Jokes are wrong because life is a serious matter. The body is the enemy. Music is wrong because it is sensuous. All is wrong!

If a man is eating healthily, he does not indulge in eating. If he is enjoying his food he does not indulge, he does not eat too much. In fact because he loves his body, he loves his food, and he remains very careful. To stuff the body too much is not the sign of a lover of the body, it is a sign of the enemy. The body can be killed in two ways: either by starvation or by over-stuffing it—but both are the ways of enmity. The lover of the body, one who respects his body as his God's gift, cannot do either. He will neither fast nor indulge in food.

And the same is true about sex and about everything.

Indulgence is created by the priests because they create repression. Once you create repression people start indulging. The more a desire is repressed, the more it wants to assert itself. It becomes mad, it becomes aggressive!

When it is allowed its natural flow, when it is accepted, when there is no fight with it, there comes a balance.

And the man who enjoys his food never eats too much; he cannot, it is impossible. Have you ever come across wild animals who are fat? Now, nobody is teaching them naturopathy, dieting or fasting. You never come across a fat wild animal.

We are deliberately saying wild animal; we are not talking about the zoos, because it is different in zoos. The animals start imitating man. In zoos you can find fat and ugly animals, but not in the wild state. Why?—because an animal simply loves, enjoys his body, eats to the point where the body is satisfied, not a bit more.

And yes, sometimes it happens that the animal fasts too, but not according to any religious rules. If he feels that the body is in such a state that it cannot take food, he is ill, and it is harmful to load the body— these are natural instincts, prompts from the spirit within—he does not eat. Sometimes even the animal may try to vomit, to unburden. A dog will go and eat grass; that helps him to vomit. And you cannot persuade him to eat till he becomes healthy again. These are natural instincts or prompts from the resident spirit.

Priests have contaminated man so much that he has forgotten all his natural instincts. Now he lives by memorized ideas. He has to fast because he follows a certain philosophy of fasting. He does not listen to the body; the body is hungry and he fasts. And then sometimes the body is not hungry at all and he eats. He goes on losing contact with his body and the spirit that runs that body.

Memory is only a part of the mind. It is the archive or store-room of the mind. And whatever the mind stores in memory is supplied by the senses. The priest conditions us to live in the archive or memory. By so doing, we completely ignore what the senses are telling us. The body is hungry and, instead of feeding it, we present it with the fasting idea pulled from the archive. But the body cannot be fed with such stupidities. We need to come out of our archives into the pooling area where the senses meet the mind. The gate connecting the senses to the mind must be re-opened. For more on this, see the author's book: The Second Birth. The Mind Is A Bag. How Loaded Is Yours? Trafford Publishing, Canada.

The body is beautiful and divine. Let's come back to the body. Let the body become alive again, and it will take care; we need not worry about it. The body has a built-in program to keep us healthy, alive, vibrant, young and fresh. The body has a built-in program and we need not learn anything about it from books and teachings.

Let us close this section with a review of the four phases in man's life:

From 0 to 7 years: At this stage, the child is self-centered and auto-sexual. When the child is born he is a narcissist. He knows and loves only his body. By just sucking his own thumb, he is in such euphoria. By playing with his own body, such as taking his toe into his mouth, he makes a circle of energy. When the child takes his toe into the mouth a circle is created and his energy starts moving in a circle. The spirit circulates naturally in the child and he enjoys, because when the spirit circulates there is great joy inside.

The child plays with his own sexual organs not knowing they are sexual organs. He has not yet been conditioned; he knows his body as one whole. And certainly, the sexual organs are the most sensitive part of his body. He utterly enjoys touching them, playing with them.

And here is where the society, the poisonous society, enters into the mind of the child: "Don't touch!" "Don't" is the first dirty, four-letter word. And out of this one four-letter word comes many more: can't, won't—these are all four-letter words. The child is told "Don't!" and the angry parent, mother or father takes child's hand away from his genitals, which are naturally very sensitive. He really enjoys it, and he is not being sexual or anything. It is just the most sensitive part of his body, the most alive part of his body, that's all.

But our minds have been conditioned! He is touching a sexual organ? That is bad, and we take his hand away. We create guilt in the child.

Now we have started destroying his natural sexuality, poisoning the original source of his joy, and creating hypocrisy in him. He will become a diplomat. When the parents are there he will not play with his genitals. The first lie has entered and he cannot be true. Now he knows that if he is true to himself, if he respects himself, if he respects his own joy, if he respects his own instinct or spirit, then the parents are angry. And he is helpless against them, he is dependent on them, his survival is with them. If they renounce him, he will be dead; so the question is of choosing whether he wants to live. The condition is that if he wants to live he has to be against himself, and the child has to yield.

The child is the most exploited person in the world. No other class has been so exploited as the child. He cannot do anything: he cannot make unions to fight with the parents, he cannot go to the court, and he cannot go to the government. He has no way to protect himself against the parental attacks.

And when the parents stop him, they are stopping him because of their own conditioning; their parents had done the same to them. They are very much embarrassed by the child's touching his own genital organs and playing with them, and so unashamedly.

Now the child knows nothing of shame, he is innocent. The "don't" has entered; the energy or spirit recoils. The first trauma has happened. Now the child will never be able to accept his sexuality naturally, joyously. Repression has happened and the child is divided in two; his body is no more whole. Some part of the body is not acceptable, some part of the body is ugly, some part of the body is unworthy to be part of his body; he rejects it. Deep down in his mind he starts castrating himself, and the spirit recoils. The spirit will not be flowing as naturally as it used to flow before this "don't" happened.

And the natural outcome of this stupidity that has been perpetually practiced on humanity is that the child is no more a natural being, hypocrisy has entered. He has to hide something from the parents or he has to feel guilty.

Many people remain stuck at this auto-sexual phase of life. That's why so much masturbation continues all over the world. It is a natural state. It would have passed on its own, it was a growing phase, but the parents disturbed the spirit's growth surge.

The child becomes stuck: he wants to play with his genitals and he cannot. Repressing, repressing, one day it is too much and he is possessed by the sexual energy. And once he has started masturbating, it may become a habit, a mechanical habit, and then he will never move to the second stage.

And the people who are responsible are the parents, the priests, and the politicians.

Now a man may remain stuck at this stage, which is very childish. He will never attain to full grown-up sexuality. He will never come to know the bliss that can come only to a grown-up sexual being. And the irony is that these are the same people who condemn masturbation and make much fuss about it. And they make such statements that are very dangerous: they have been telling people that if you masturbate you will go blind, if you masturbate you will become a zombie, if you masturbate you will never be intelligent, you will remain stupid. Now all the scientific findings are agreed upon one point: that masturbation never harms anybody. But these suggestions harm. All the psychological researches agree that masturbation never harms anybody. It is a natural outlet of energy. But these ideas—that you will go blind—may make it dangerous to your eyes, because again and again you will think that you will go blind, that you will go blind, that you will go blind.... So many people are using glasses, and the reason may not be in the eyes; the reason may be just somewhere else. So many millions of people are stupid, and the reason may not be that they are stupid—because no child is born stupid, all children are born intelligent. The reason may be somewhere else: in these baseless, negative suggestions. And so many people are afraid, trembling continuously, have no trust in themselves, no self-confidence, are continuously afraid, because they know what they have been doing—masturbating.

We repeat: masturbation has never harmed anybody. But the moment when a person masturbates is a very sensitive and delicate moment; his whole being is open and flowing. In that moment if some suggestion is dropped in his mind—and he himself will drop the suggestion, "Now what if I go mad? if I go blind? if I remain always stupid?"—these constant auto-hypnotic suggestions are the cause of a thousand and one illnesses, of a thousand and one psychological problems and perversions.

Who is responsible for this? The parents, priests and politicians!

If the child is allowed the natural phase of auto-sexuality, he moves on his own to the second phase, the homosexual—but very few people move to the second phase. The majority remain with the first phase.

From 7 to 14 years: The child becomes eccentric, a great questioner and a homosexual. Few people move to this second and natural phase. The child loves his body. If the child is a boy, he loves a boy's body, his body. To jump to a woman's body, to a girl's body, would be too much of a big gap. Naturally, first he moves in love with other boys; or if the child is a girl, the first natural instinct is to love other girls because they have the same kind of body, the same kind of being. She can understand the girls better than the boys; boys are a world apart.

The homosexual phase is a natural phase, the phase of true friendship. There, society helps people to remain stuck again, because it creates barriers between man and woman, girls and boys. If those barriers are not there, then soon the homosexual phase fades away; the interest starts shifting into the hetero-sex, the other sex. But for that, society does not give chances—a great wall is put between the boy and the girl. In the schools they have to sit apart or they have to be educated separately. In the colleges they have to live in separate hostels. Their meeting, their being together, is not accepted.

Homosexuality is perpetuated by the society and condemned by the same society. These strategies have to be understood. The same society condemns the homosexual, calls him perverted, criminal. And it is the same society that creates it!

We place man and woman in watertight compartments. And when the man wants to love he cannot find a woman, and the woman wants to love and she cannot find a man. Then, whatsoever is available will do. She starts falling in love with a woman and he starts falling in love with a man. And it is not satisfying either, but it is better than nothing. Nature has to find its way. If you don't allow the natural course, it will find some roundabout way. Otherwise homosexuality is a natural phase; it passes by itself.

From 14 to 49 years: This is the hetero-sexual phase. Sex arises at fourteen and the child is interested in the other sex. The hetero-sexual phase lasts till the age of forty-nine years. Sex energy is on the ascendant from 14-35 years of age. The period of 14-21 years is torrid, with ambition and adventure coming up during the period of 21-28 years. At 27 years a balanced hetero-sexual attitude arises if we let the sex energy flow naturally. We transcend the touch and go aspect of heterosexuality. It is time to settle down in security and comfort. It is time for marriage to a partner. Hankering after sex is now history. A partner is enough and perfectly okay. Love can now happen because the man and woman are mentally and sexually mature! For love to happen, the man and the woman must be mentally and sexually mature. They must have gone beyond the first two stages and the torrid stage of heterosexuality; only then can love happen. And very rarely are there people who are mature men and mature women. So nothing happens; they make love, but that love is only superficial. Deep down they are auto-sexual or homo-sexual. At the most, they are at the torrid hetero-sexual stage.

The torrid hetero-sexual phase is a natural phase, the phase of know-ing what the other sex looks like. This is the phase where a man can make love with a woman all-night-long, till-day-break (TDB). The bliss of sex is such that a man feels no sleep and has an almost permanent erection without taking any aphrodisiac. My people say: i-solu ütö örü, i-gbajie amü. (If you follow the bliss of sex, you will break your penis) But there again, society helps people to remain stuck, because it reinforces the existing barriers between man and woman, girls and boys. Sex for adolescents in the 14-21 years age bracket is called defile-ment, punishable by imprisonment of the boy. If those barriers are not there, then soon the torrid hetero-sexual phase fades away; the interest starts shifting into the consolidation phase, the marriage phase. Our high divorce rates result from the bungled implementation of the torrid hetero-sexual phase. We jump hurriedly into marriage, only to hanker after the hetero-sexuality we ought to have transcended. The women out there that I do not know must be different from the wife I know. If the torrid hetero-sex phase is allowed its natural course we transcend the tendency to jump from one partner to the other.

Torrid hetero-sexuality is perpetuated by the society and condemned by the same society. The same society condemns the torrid hetero-sex-ual, calls him perverted, criminal. And it is the same society that cre-ates it! The dirty old man and woman run after mates who could be their children, simply because they failed to complete the torrid het-ero-sexual phase before jumping into marriage. The married woman hides behind religion in order to complete an uncompleted torrid het-ero-sex phase. Religious and social conditioning prevented her from going through the natural phases of life. She is sexually repressed and the various religious retreats and all-night religious vigils provide pro-pitious terrain to catch up on lost ground. We can always steal a snatch behind the statue of some saint or on some remote corner of the angel field! You just need to be smart. Because she did not experience certain phases of life, she would not tolerate her children experiencing them. If she did not experience the torrid hetero-sex phase, then no child of hers should even try it. Ogene Ïkpaachï Agukwu Nrï says: Ife onye e-meghi n'okolobia o-mee na-nka. (Whatever you fail to do in your youth, you will do in your old age) ·

The torrid hetero-sex phase is dangerous because of the diseases associated with promiscuity and the risk of unwanted pregnancy. But the knowledge of the menstrual cycle was basic in the upbringing of the woman. Our grandmothers knew when it was safe to have sex without getting pregnant. They associated their periods of ovulation with the phases of the moon. They listened to their bodies and watched the phases of the moon. Sexual hygiene boils down to washing the genitals with clean water after sexual intercourse.

Having settled down at the age of 28 years the mature couple accept themselves as they are and love develops naturally. They get into marriage for the same reason: to build a family. They are all for the government, rules, regulations and discipline. From 42-49 years of age, our energies start declining, we are interested in religion, and sex subsides. Soon the hetero-sexual phase fades away entirely; the interest starts shifting into the celibacy phase, the no-sex phase.

From 49-56 years of age, we move inwards in meditation to find the God within all of us. Then the fourth and ultimate phase, celibacy, comes. This is real celibacy; not the celibacy of the monks—that is not celibacy at all—but the celibacy of enlightened men and women. Sex has disappeared; you don't need the outer woman, you don't need the outer man. Now your inner man and woman have fallen into a union, and this union is not momentary. This is real marriage; your mind and spirit are welded together. The spirit inundates the mind and body. Now to be orgasmic is your natural state. An enlightened person lives in orgasm continuously; he breathes in and out in orgasm. In the period of 56-63 years of age, we withdraw from all social entanglements. From 63-70 years of age a re-birth of the mind takes place and we become as little children: self-centered. We achieve the goal of incarnation: to unite the mortal mind with the immortal spirit and become as the legendary winged globe. We become as one of the Gods! The program for this re-birth of the mind is described in the author's book, "The Second Birth. The Mind Is A Bag. How Loaded Is Yours?" Next, we move further inwards, ready to die at the age of 70 years.

The above are the four stages of sex.

A man who has repressed his sexuality for his whole life will go mad on seeing a naked woman, because it will be like an explosion in his being. But a man who has not repressed any sexuality will not even take any note of seeing a naked woman; or he may simply think, "What a beautiful body!"—and that is that. He does not want to grab or possess it. This was the case with my ancestors before Christianity came. Just as we look at a rose flower: the rose flower is naked, and we don't put clothes on the rose flower. We don't put clothes on the animals.

While picking pepper in her garden, my granduncle's wife had seen me through her fence fumbling a girl's breasts. The girl and I were sitting behind the Obi and facing her compound. I was on the point of putting one of her nipples into my mouth when she cleared her throat behind the thick fence foliage. The girl quickly hid her breasts and we escaped. The old lady called me later and jocularly asked: Nwa m, ï na-elikwu nli-nwa gböö? My son, do you also eat baby food? As I seemed not to understand, she added: Ï-mara na ife ï-chölü ï-sünye n'önü mg-bee bü nli-nwa? Ï ka-bü nwa? Don't you know that what you wanted to put into your mouth a while ago is called baby food? Are you still a baby? We laughed and I left her. I did not fully understand at that time, because a woman's breasts always fascinate. The sexually repressed youth would go haywire in front the naked breasts of a girl. But the lesson was clear: why should a boy still be grabbing and sucking a woman's breasts? That's something for babies!

Whom do we think we are deceiving with our repressions? Our repressions are bound to take revenge on us from the back door. The whole hypocrisy can disappear from the world if sex is accepted naturally. Ninety-nine percent of hypocrisy is dependent on sex-repression.

Now, religions go on giving us double-binds. They first say, "Be authentic, be true," and all that they teach makes us inauthentic, untrue, hypocrites. This is a double-bind. They say, "Believe in truth, believe in God"; now this is a double-bind. Belief simply means you don't know and still you are believing; it is untrue. If one has to be true, one has to seek and search and only then believe. But they say, "First believe in God, and then you will be able to find Him." But to begin with belief is to begin with a lie.

And God is truth, and we begin in lies. Life is truth, and we begin in hypocrisy. If we go on missing, it is no wonder. We are bound to miss all joy.

In the past, this antagonism towards sex has been exploited for one more reason. First, the priest exploited it to make us afraid, to make us tremble. Then he became very haughty, holier than others; he dominated everybody. And the politician exploited it in another way, for some other reason: if sex is repressed, man becomes violent. Now, again this is a scientific finding. If sex is repressed man becomes violent; violence is a perversion of sexual energy. Now, the politicians needed armies, violent people, murderers. The only way to get so many murderers was to repress sex.

If you don't repress sex, who wants to kill? For what? The sword, the dagger, the bayonet are nothing but phallic deep down. The man wanted to penetrate the woman's body and it would have been a beautiful phenomenon if it had happened in love; but it could not happen, it was not allowed. Now he is mad, he wants to enter anybody's body, in any way—with a dagger, with a sword, with a bayonet.

Sex has been repressed and the politician exploited it in his own way. He needed armies. He needed slaves ready to die or to kill. The person who has not lived his life in celebration is ready to die for anything. He is ready to become a martyr for any stupid idea, ideology, scripture, or religion.

The man who has lived the joy and the blessings of a life will not be so easily ready to die. He will say, "Why? Life is so precious. I cannot sacrifice my life just for a piece of cloth called the national flag." "I cannot sacrifice my life," he will say, "just because somebody has burned the Koran. So what? Print another." "I cannot sacrifice my life because somebody has burned a temple. So what? My life is more precious than your temple, because my body is the temple of a living God." But a man who has not loved and who has not lived is always ready. When life is misery it is better to die; any excuse is enough. The politician needed violence; he exploited sexual repression. The priest needed power; he exploited sexual repression.

Up to now no revolution has happened, because ninety-nine percent of hypocrisy, untruth, exploitation, and violence depend on sexual repression, and no sexual revolution has yet happened.

A repressed mind is an obsessed mind. It cannot see reality as it is; it is impossible. Before a repressed man can see reality as it is, he will have to drop all kinds of repressions. A clean mind is needed, an innocent mind is needed.

Man has lived with hypocrisy.

And remember, sex may look like mud, but it contains the lotus flower in it. Sex contains bliss, because life is God. We must move from sex to enlightenment or a re-birth of the mind; this is the only natural and rightful way. We should not get stuck anywhere in sex. Transcendence of sex comes through sex itself. And the people who are teaching repression are not teaching transcendence. In fact, they go on pouring more mud on us. They go on forcing us deeper in the mud because there is no possibility of transcendence if we have not moved through these sexual stages of auto-eroticism, homo-eroticism, hetero-eroticism, and then to transcendence. And the lotus blooms resulting in the second birth. Avoid the priests and the politicians and you can achieve it. They are standing in the way.

But they always wanted it this way. It is good for them; it is not good for anybody else. They have diverted our love. They have taken its natural object from us; then love can be diverted. Now there are people who are in love with the motherland—what foolishness! What do we mean by "motherland"? There are people who are in love with the fatherland—still more foolish. There are people who are in love with countries, ideologies—communism, fascism, and cultism.

Our natural object of love has been taken away; now our love is frantically searching for anything to become tethered to. If the natural object of love is taken away, one will love money or one may even love his umbrella. One may start falling in love with things: one may start falling in love with flags, countries. All kinds of nonsense is possible once the natural love is distracted.

Let us bring our love back to its natural object—sex. Let our love have a spontaneity of its own; let us allow it to take possession of us, and we will be transformed through it. Sex, when transcended, transmutes into love. And love or sex transcendence as described above is the secret key to mental regeneration, re-birth or enlightenment.

THE BASICS OF ÖDÏNANÏ

Some Igbo tell me that Ödïnanï can only be practiced in the village where the ritual ingredients are readily available. But I disagree because Ödïnanï is a philosophy, and every philosophy is primarily mental before becoming practical. Once we understand the Ödïnanï philosophy, the ritual aspect of it is easily adaptable to environments and circumstances: we cook our food with the firewood at our disposal. Nkü ndï nwelü be fa na-eghelü fa ite. The wife who wants to embrace her husband uses the hands at her disposal, her hands. It is the emotion attached to such gestures that personalize them and render them unique. The same is true of Ödïnanï.

Our ancestors knew that God (Chineke) or Universal Spirit was either incarnate in forms or free. They also knew that the God who governed the planet Earth (Anï) is more powerful than the God who governed the human body (Chi). The God who governs the human body (Chi) is an entity, while the God who governs the Earth is a hierarchized Army or Host of entities having the same origin as the entity that animates man. Religion is a desire to commune with a spirit that is superior to ours. We admire the Nature around us, convinced that the fashioning Gods are truly powerful. This is the origin of man's reverence for the Gods of Nature. Our wise ancestors venerated God in Nature. They found God in themselves (Chi), in the earth on which they walked (Anï), in the water, in the air, in the fire, in the trees, etc, and in all living things.

Man's mind (Uche) sleeps and wakes. The spirit (Chi) rests only at the body's death. During sleep the heart beats, the blood circulates, the food is digested, the wastes are eliminated, etc., the spirit (Chi) keeps watch and directs the operations; but thinking (echiche) has ceased and the mind is asleep. When we wake from sleep the mind takes the front seat, while the spirit moves into the background to continue its ceaseless maintenance of the body and the mind.

Man's nearest God is his Chi. Next come the Chi of his parents and ancestors. Next in line is the Chi of the planet Earth, Anï. Note that Anï comprises all the Alüshï and Spirit Guilds on Earth. Thereafter come the Chi of the other planets in our solar system. Finally come the Chi of the Sun (Anyanwü) and Its Hosts, at the apex of the Hierarchy that governs our solar system.

In the village, as anywhere else, we live on the Earth. The Gods of the Earth are thus available and accessible everywhere on the planet. We may, therefore, venerate and call on them everywhere on the planet. The Moslem may touch the Earth with his forehead in Lagos or at the North Pole. I can pour my libation by pouring water or wine on the ground in Awka or any other corner of the world. All depends on the why of these gestures. By touching the Earth with my forehead during prayer, I yoke myself onto the Gods of the Earth. The libation that I pour on the ground is an offering to the Gods of the Earth.

Thus, Ödïnanï can be practiced anywhere on Earth. Take the example of a student who lives in a hostel or in an apartment in the city. How can he manage practicing Ödïnanï basics? The starting point is for him to note that it is his spirit or God (Chi) who watches over the health of his body and mind. His Chi is his share of Universal Omnipotence. He should trust his Chi and then appreciate Its power. He will thus start to increase his awareness and express more gratitude to his Chi.

Next he may look for external support to supplement his weaknesses. He may thus appeal to the Gods of the Earth (Anï). Let him take a cup of water, isolate himself a bit, remove his shoes, clearly mur-

mur his desires for the attention of those Gods, pour the content of the cup on the ground or into a kitchen or bathroom sink at the end of his prayer. The magic is mental and the gesture with the water simply reinforces the mental imagery. He should read Psalm 139 and view it as a situation where the mind expresses its gratitude to its God. Let him discover his God through mental silence. This is the goal of meditation and yoga. When he passes his examinations and obtains his certificates, let him not forget to celebrate his God (Chi) and the Gods who supported him. The birthday anniversary should celebrate the God (Chi) of the celebrator. Alas, this Eucharist feast now celebrates a date!

A friend survived a ghastly motor accident. Instead of celebrating the event with his Chi and loved ones, he rushed to the church to donate money to Chineke: tüö mma-mma n'ünöüka. As though Chineke, the Great Giver, needed anything! He invited me to the special church service but I stayed home and was frank with him. I asked him how he hoped to get anything from Chineke when he ignores his Chi or share of that Chineke. I told him that he was deluded and had mortgaged his reason to the priests.

I repeat: Ödïnanï is a philosophy, which is primarily mental before becoming practical. Once we understand the Ödïnanï philosophy, the ritual aspect of it is easily adaptable to environments and circumstances: we cook our food with the firewood at our disposal. Nkü onye nwelü be ya na-eghelü ya ite. The hierarchy of subservience in Ödïnanï is: my Chi, Ndï Ichie (dead as well as living male and female parents), Alüshï and Anï. This is the Igbo mindset that colonialism has strived to destroy through the impracticable monotheism of Christianity. There are Gods and the Christian God is one of them, period. Mentally reclaim your Gods and be free again. Venerate and worship Anï and Its Gods wherever you are on the surface of Anï. Walk barefoot whenever you can to keep contact with Anï. Shrines and temples are embellishments in the practice of Ödïnanï. If you can afford them, fine. Otherwise, don't bother about them. The magic of Ödïnanï is first of all mental before its concretization in visible phenomena.

3
TALISMANS, ÖGWÜ, ÖTÜMÖKPÖ, ÖKPÖ, JAZZ, JUJU

WHAT ARE THESE PSYCHO-SPIRITUAL OBJECTS?

On whatever level of embodied being the same controlling power—Life or Spirit—presides over the phenomena of experience. The Ancients tell us that certain Gods presided over marketplaces and others over battlefields—an idea long supposed to have been abandoned as empty superstition. Nevertheless there are Gods, Angels or Divine presiding powers, both of marketplaces and of battlefields, Gods, in fact, having a special and controlling relationship to all the phenomena of the Cosmos. Such Gods are entirely real; and the phenomena we know, as well as many more that we do not know, owe their being and their peculiar form to the presidency or participation of those Gods. These Gods are simply modalities of the one God called Life. Electricity, magnetism, attraction and repulsion are all modalities or aspects of a unique power—Life. Moreover it is on a knowledge of the Gods concerned in any given object or event that practical occultism depends for its power.

Constantly surrounded by dangers and things he cannot understand, man always had the need to believe. Man believed in the magical, supernatural, protective powers of certain religious objects. Sacred objects, Talismans and Pentacles, with their engraved or drawn symbols and the God or power they are supposed to represent, have always been considered as a tangible link between man and the Absolute. That their use has survived the passage of time is proof of their efficacy, because man always abandons anything that has not proved its worth. But man believed in these objects and, given the positive results obtained, continues to believe in them. Being a psycho-spiritual support, the talisman implies faith.

But this faith is more or less developed in all of us and it is our duty, in our quest for happiness, to intensify and use it to the maximum. All civilizations have had faith in their religious objects; but your task henceforth is to have faith in yourself (your Spirit), because a talisman is simply an aid, a "crutch for the one-legged person," a stage in the recognition of your own powers. Unfortunately, man always wants to see in order to believe. Indeed, this immovable and inflexible faith in ourselves is difficult to maintain, particularly in the beginning when the expected results are slow in coming.

To strongly believe in our own potentials without prior concrete results, constitutes a very abstract exercise for the mind. That is why all religions resort to objects of worship in order to concretize the faith of their followers in a material object that they can see and touch.

For those who have no religion, for those who cannot sufficiently believe without some material aid, for those whose faith is weak, magic or spiritual wisdom provides the seeker with a set of instruments and aids designed to support his will and materialize his mental images; among these objects, talismans and pentacles are the most widespread.

The Ancients tell us: "Whether the object of your faith is true or false, you will obtain the same results." Thus, whether your faith is founded on the bones of a dead saint, on the healing power of some waters (Lourdes, Nwangene), on a sacred picture (pentacle), on an object (talisman, amulet, gris-gris, juju, ötümökpö, ökpö, jazz, etc.), you will obtain the same results solely by the powerful suggestion given to your own Spirit.

A talisman is not, as many believe, a mascot or good-luck-charm; it is simply a condenser of psychic fluid, which must be helped by personal effort. The sole aim of the talisman is to support and facilitate the effort of its owner, at the required time. The talisman only represents a concrete extension of your intention. Because, back of every talisman is a mental image of some desired goal—money, prestige, pull, protection from mishap, etc.

Take the wrestling talisman called "aba e-lu ana" (back-no-touch-ground!). A black cat would be a key item in the preparation of this talisman. The Dibïa will impress the wrestler's mind with a peculiar characteristic of this animal: it never falls on its back! He will secure the cat with a rope and then throw it into the air. The animal will come down on its feet before the eyes of the wrestler. With this strong mental image in his mind and the resulting talisman in his pocket, the wrestler in the arena transmutes into a cat. Through sympathetic magic, he displays all the characteristics of the animal. Note that the wrestler knows the art and has trained. The talisman simply gives him a spiritual edge.

No talisman, no matter how elaborate it may be, can bring you anything if, from the start, you lack the firm will and the ardent desire to succeed. The talisman simply helps you to keep the mind on the object of your desire, to conserve a strong will and your faith in yourself. But he who carries a talisman without understanding its meaning and goal is like a child holding a book on nuclear physics.

Ready-made talismans have as much spiritual value as any other object, as long as the purchaser places all his faith and hopes in them. This explains why these ready-made talismans are expensive. Because the makers know that the more difficult it is for a purchaser to mobilize the required sum, the greater will be his tendency to believe in their "miraculous" qualities. At the time when their desires are obtained, people do not attribute such success to their own faith in themselves but to the miracle-object or talisman.

It is evident that these objects become efficacious when their users concentrate their faith in them. This is the whole secret of their "miraculous virtues"; it is imperative that the users believe in them, with conviction and perseverance. Since it is clear that one cannot truly believe what one does not understand, it is imperative that the user of a pentacle should know the exact meaning of the various symbols inscribed on it (the meaning and desired goal). Talismans have virtue and efficacy only when they are in perfect correspondence with their owner. A talisman has no value unless its owner understands it. You have to understand it. If you tell a good Dibïa Ögwü that his ögwü is not efficacious (ögwü gï a-dïrö ile), he asks: Ï makwa ka e shi-eji ögwü? Do you know how to handle a talisman?

As soon as the owner of a talisman understands its meaning and goal, mental imagery becomes more precise and mental creation follows the desired orientation; the will to succeed and persistent faith will procure the desired goal. Believe in the power of your talisman, for this helps a lot in the beginning. Later, when you have mastered how to use your creative visualization skills and appreciated the tangible results obtained by trust in your own spirit (Chi), try to do away with your talisman.

USE OF TALISMANS

The best place to keep a talisman is where you will see it periodically. Each time it comes to your attention, you will consciously or unconsciously formulate the goal that you have set yourself to achieve. During those moments, make an effort to mentally materialize your secret desire. Only a periodic repetition of your creative mental images can bring about the materialization of your desire. This is why the makers of talismans request us to do certain daily rituals (i-lekwa ögwü). A talisman may require a prayer to be said upon it on waking in the morning and before talking to anybody. At the end of the prayer, we are requested to clearly state our desired goal, say, seven times. The daily ritual simply helps to produce vivid mental images of the desired goal, which we let go into space at the end of the ritual. This is also the secret behind the Psalms we are asked to recite daily at appointed hours, with a view to achieving some objective. The Psalms help to vivify the mental images, while their daily repetition at appointed hours helps to hasten the outward manifestation of the images. It is all sympathetic or natural magic of reaping in the outside world the seeds that you have sown in your mental world (your mental creations).

If each time you remember your talisman, you mentally affirm the approaching realization of your goal, you have succeeded. It has played its role, because by the periodic mental realization of your desire, the latter will finally materialize. Do not forget that your talisman alone cannot have any tangible effect. It is there simply to help you, but the principal effort must come from you.

Once you have used a talisman, preserve it preciously or burn it. According to tradition, the talisman looses its virtue if it is lent or alienated; one should be very careful in doing away with one's talisman, because it could be used as a weapon against its previous owner (bewitchment, etc.)—it contains your personal magnetism, condensed! When you will have succeeded in using your own Spirit to achieve a number of goals that you set for yourself, you will become conscious of the immense power that lies asleep within you. From this point onward, you will only need your creative imaginations and you can throw away your talismans. They would have, at least, helped you to start off and then assert yourself. They would have served their purpose and that, truly, is not a bad job!

On creative imaginations, the reader will find all the works in my book "The Second Birth. The Mind Is A Bag. How Loaded Is Yours? What follows is taken from that book.

Contemplation or Visualization: Having learned to concentrate the attention on mental images, the mind should train itself to contemplate or visualize such images for as long as it desires; contemplation is sustained concentration.

Contemplation or visualization consists in forming and holding a mental image of things and conditions as you wish them to be in actuality. The mental image tends to create for itself a material and objective form and existence—it is the mental pattern around which the material conditions tend to group themselves. It is, in fact, the seed-form of the thing itself. The prime factor in visualization is to create a clear mental image of the thing or condition desired, as if it were actually existent at that moment. Visualization is the creative process employed by those desiring to manifest mental images on the mental and material planes. These three rules of visualization should be observed: (1) See yourself as you wish to be. (2) See others as you wish them to be. (3) See conditions as you wish them to be. Around these visualized ideals, do the material realities form and crystallize.

Visualization is a critical stage in the process of mental creation. The secret of mental creation may be simply stated as the art of mental imaging, backed by the will. Mental creation, under any name, may be found to consist of simply the power to create strong, clear mental images, and to project them into the outer world by means of the concentrated will.

Whether you desire to influence people or events, the principle is the same: the projection of your mental image into objectivity, and the materializing of that picture by the operation of the law of attraction.

Let us use an analogy as an aid to understanding the mechanics of mental creation. A slide projector kit comprises a slide projector and a perpendicular flat screen. The slide projector is an opto-mechanical device to view photographic slides. It has four main elements: a fan-cooled electric light bulb or other light source, a reflector and condensing lens to direct the light to the slide, a holder for the slide and a focusing lens. Light passes through the transparent slide and focusing lens, and the resulting image is enlarged and projected onto a perpendicular flat screen.

Thus, the three key elements of the slide projector kit are: concentrated light, a slide containing an image, and a perpendicular flat screen.

For mental creation, the concentrated light represents the polarized attention; the slide containing the picture represents the mental image held in the mind; the perpendicular flat surface represents the objective world. Let us then fix the symbol of the slide projector kit firmly in our minds, and recall it whenever we practice mental creation. By holding this mechanism in mind, we will be able to give increased force, power and reality to the projection of mental images.

With this symbol still in mind, we see that the power and strength of the projected image depends materially upon the strength and focused force of the light falling on the slide. If the light is weak, or dim, or flickering, the projected image will be likewise. And, if the rays of the light are not focused and concentrated properly, the force and power of the light will not be properly directed and applied. Therefore, in mental creations, we must hold our polarized attention firmly concentrated upon the mental image. This is why contemplation or visualization is very important.

Likewise, if the slide containing the picture—the mental image—is poorly and faintly drawn, the projected image will also be faulty; in fact, the fault will be more apparent, for it will be magnified according to the distance to which it is projected. Therefore, cultivate the art of mental imaging and endeavor to train your imagination to see clearly that which you wish to project into the objective world for the purpose of materialization. Train your imagination to form and hold plain, clear pictures of the things and conditions that you wish to materialize in the objective world. Upon this one thing depends much of the efficacy and success of the process of mental creation. If you cannot fill in the details of your mental picture at first, at least draw firm, strong general outlines, and add the details later before projecting.

HELP YOURSELF, FOR THE GODS HELP ONLY THOSE WHO HELP THEMSELVES

You want to be of some account in the world: in your profession or in your trade! Begin to play-act the part. Live it! Make it a part of yourself. It is up to you to begin to move the life-forces in your favor, for nobody else will do it for you. Imagine yourself as being what you want to be, and the faith or trust—in your spirit—behind this imaginative effort will materialize your image of yourself. The job you desired, the rank you wished to attain, the post you wanted to fill, the role you longed to act—all these will be yours if you act them in trust and in complete earnestness of purpose and with no doubt in your mind.

Note that to desire the position of a company's accountant, one must first study and qualify as an accountant. Why dream of a job for which one is not prepared? We must always work as nature does—no short-cuts! Prepare the trenches and wait in trust for the rains to fill them with water. Do your part and trust your spirit (Chi) to crown your effort, by the materialization of your legitimate desire.

WORDS HAVE POWER

Consider the statement: "I'm now eating a lemon". Imagine it, i.e., create a clear mental picture of the lemon-eating! What happens? Your mouth is full of saliva trying to wash away the lemon that you are not actually eating. The lemon-eating image created by the mind triggers the intervention of the spirit, which "asks" the salivary glands to wash the lemon away. Thus word-images do not just reflect reality; they create reality, like the flow of saliva. Eat a lemon if you have never done so and try the exercise some days later. When you have licked a piece of lemon, then you "know" the taste of it and you can imagine the lemon-eating very easily.

As adults, we dull our appetite for life with negative words, and the words, gathering power with repetition, in turn create negative lives, for which our appetites become dulled.

"How are you?"

"Ah—can't complain", or "No use complaining", or "Not too bad".

How does the spirit within respond to these dreary views? Is it a "pain in the neck" to do the dishes? Remember that the spirit is no subtle interpreter and takes you at your word. It says, "This fellow is asking for a pain in the neck. Okay. A pain in the neck is coming up."

Of course, every time that we say something gives us a pain, a pain does not immediately result. Simply because no clear mental image is associated with the terrible words we ignorantly use. The spirit takes little note of empty words—words not put into images. The spirit ensures that the body's natural state is good health, and all its processes are geared toward health. In time, though, with enough verbal pounding away at its defenses and careless imagination by the mind, it delivers up the very illnesses we order.

AFFIRMATIONS

Affirmations are positive assertions of the existence of the conditions which you wish to bring about. They tend to aid the visualization to a great degree, and besides have a power of their own. Always use statements as in the present tense. Do not say to yourself, "Such and such a thing will be bye and bye," but boldly assert "Such and such a thing is existent and in actual being, now, this moment." The power of the positive statement must be experienced in order to be appreciated.

Make your statements earnestly and positively—avoid all half-hearted statements, for they result in half-hearted results. In making your statements, do not use a tone of entreaty or of asking a favor—speak in a tone of command. Of course, these statements should not be made aloud for other people to hear. They have the best effect when made in a state of meditation and concentration—in Alpha or deeper levels of consciousness. Use them in connection with visualization, and you will find that they will tend to energize and vitalize your mental images.

DENIALS

Denials are negative forms of affirmations. They have a most positive effect when rightly used. With the individual whose attention is polarized, he is able to exert much power by boldly denying out of existence the obstacles and difficulties which beset his path. It is marvelous, at times, to see how the obstructing things show a tendency to disintegrate and disappear from one's mental world, which is followed later by a response of like kind and degree in the material world. Do not be afraid to say: "I deny this or that obstacle. It has no power over me. I deny it out of my world. For me it does not exist." My folks would say: Ügbüü! Not for me, I have slipped away! Ö bülü ögwü na o-lere! If it is magic, it has failed! Make your denials as positive as your affirmations. Command, don't beg or implore.

Your spirit is your personal guardian. It needs clear instructions from you and takes you at your word. So, make your assertions in a tone of command; don't beg or implore.

PROJECTION OF MENTAL IMAGES INTO THE OUTSIDE WORLD

Projection: The mind will project its creations or images into the outside world by contemplating them and simply withdrawing its attention from them. The materialization in the outside world is the job of the spirit—resident and universal.

Attention is the spirit component of the human mind. By concentrating the attention on a mental image the mind pulls in extra supply of spirit into itself and pours it into the image. And contemplation of a mental image further floods the image with spirit.

To project or radiate the image into space we must end the contemplation by withdrawing attention from it, trusting that our spirit will materialize it in the outside world

But the projection or radiation of mental images involves the use of spirit or psychic energy, and this requires a prior condensation. The essential condition for the condensation is: accumulate your psychic energy by refusing to think of the subject that you intend to project later; the images and thoughts will come alright, but refuse to give them attention. In this manner, you will accumulate your psychic energy during the time separating two periods of projection or radiation. For example: 23 hours of spirit condensation and one hour of radiation. This is the Hermetic operation of Coagula (coagulate) and Solve (dissolve), symbolized in the Devil of the Tarot.

After contemplating and projecting, it is necessary to isolate the mind. This is achieved by diverting your attention from all images and thoughts related to the subject on which you concentrated and which you have projected. Put your attention onto anything different from the subject on which you have just concentrated. With the attention, visit the interior of your earth or body. Circulate your attention within and ignore all stimuli related to the mental image you have just projected into space. Or just sit and watch images floating across your mind—simply become a witness to your internal television. Be confident that the god or spirit that dwells in your body will take charge and conveniently materialize your mental image in the most suitable way. This rule is not only important for the mental balance of the operator, but also for the efficacy of his volition.

Do you wish to attract something? And do you think of the thing all day long and even during the night? Your attempt to attract the thing will fail! Your influence will be ineffective as a result of your attitude, because you have dissipated, minute by minute, all the psychic or life's forces that you were supposed to accumulate before radiating them under high tension. Here is the correct approach:

1. You want to attract a given result? Create a two-phased dynamism as follows:

   (a) Create and visualize a precise mental image of the desired event; this puts your spirit in the required state of magnetic attraction; and then

   (b) Let go the image by isolating the mind, i.e., by refusing attention to the subject which you have just visualized. You thus allow your own spirit, coupled with the universal spirit, to effect the magnetic attraction.

2. Do you want to avert, repel an undesirable event? Also create a two-phased dynamism as follows:

   (c) Create and contemplate a precise mental image inhibiting the undesirable event; this places your spirit in a state of magnetic repulsion; and then

   (d) Let go the inhibiting image by isolating the mind, i.e., by refusing attention to the subject which you have just visualized. You thus allow your own spirit, coupled with the universal spirit, to effect the desired magnetic repulsion.

The isolation of the mind after projection is tricky in the beginning, because it requires control of the attention. The projected mental image would naturally pop into the mind from memory and the untrained mind would resume the contemplation of an image it has just let go into space. By contemplating and projecting an image, the mind concluded its drawings and submitted them to the builder-spirit for implementation. Giving new attention later to the projected image confuses the spirit, which says: "This fellow is calling back the drawings he submitted to me for execution. Probably for some amendment! That's okay. I'll suspend implementation until he stops coming back to withdraw his drawings." The inability to isolate the mind delays the materialization of our mental creations and may even nullify our efforts. We acquire the ability to isolate the mind through patience and practice.

Here are the essential points to remember:

- Anything you desire exists in the surrounding Universe, and you can obtain it.

- Your indwelling spirit (Chi) is your share of the ambient Universal Spirit or God. Have complete trust in your own spirit, which you have now coupled with the Universal Spirit through the completion of the coagulation phase of our re-birth work program. Recall that the mind uses its spirit component—its attention—to get a hold on the indwelling and universal spirit. And that with this achievement, animal-man transmutes into god-man.

- Ask yourself if there is a single reason why you should not obtain what you desire. You will see that there is none as long as your desire is justified and merited, and this removes all doubt from your mind. Doubt creates a negative condition, disturbs the inductive power of your spirit and, as a result, hinders the physical materialization of your mental creations.

- Next, make and visualize a precise mental image of the thing you ardently desire. Let go the image by isolating the mind or by withdrawing your attention from the visualized image, and allowing your spirit to handle the materialization. Have total faith or trust in your own spirit—your god—and keep an expectant positive attitude. Do not try to foresee how the object of your desire will come to you; the universal spirit, working through your own spirit, will do the job in a convenient and just manner, without hurting anybody.

- Ask specifically and exclusively for one thing. This helps you to create a precise and clear mental picture; the clearer the picture, the faster its materialization. If you desire to have a car, do not bother about the amount of money needed to buy it. Focus on creating a clear and precise mental image of your dream car; mixing the car and its cost will have you asking for two things at a time instead of one. You desire money? How much? Imagine the exact amount!

- Spend time to formulate your mental pictures and remember that you are using an Immutable Law. Always remember the axiom: "In the universe, nothing is created and nothing is lost; all is transformation." By leaving the materialization of your mental creations in the hands of your spirit, you are simply saying to your God: Your will be done!

An old prayer to the resident spirit (Chi) runs thus:
Grant me good whether prayed for or unsought by me;
But that which I ask amiss, do thou avert.

The wisdom of this prayer is evident. It is a safety net to protect us from the snares of desire. The objects of desire are like firewood in the bush. And he who brings ant-infested firewood to his house, requests the company of lizards. Ö kpatalü nkü arürü shïlï ngwele fükwütie ölïlï. Carefully inspect and select the firewood you want to take from the bush back to your home, to be sure they contain no ants. If they contain ants, then lizards will surely visit you. You will reap whatever you have sown.

It may be fun to desire your neighbor's wife. Watch it! Your spirit will help you if you insist. It does not distinguish between our so-called "good and evil." But you are entirely on your own and soon it will not be much fun getting away from your neighbor's wife, who is now glued to you by your own magnetism.

Remember that the Spirit is neither a moralist nor a subtle interpreter. It takes your mental images and materializes them.

The male that lusts after the female exalts his spirit, through mental imagery, in order to emit magnetism capable of exerting its action as soon as favorable conditions arise.

In societies where sex is repressed for religious or other reasons, the resourceful adolescents discover the power of the spirit through apparently innocent erotic games. Sex cannot be engaged in unless a basic set of clothing is put aside. And since sex is not allowed, they keep their clothes on and play erotic games. They cuddle, kiss, and gently caress the body—particularly the back side of the body. Slowly, but surely, the resident spirit is exalted and set in motion.

The girl who, sure of herself, plays the coquette with her lover succumbs at a moment she least expects to do so. She is a victim of a natural enchantment to which she submitted by playing with an omnipotent force. Conquered by a mysterious tipsiness, she momentarily loses control, and the act which she had resolved not to participate in is accomplished. But her resolve not to participate in the sexual act is purely a mental thing, backed by a complete ignorance of how she is made and how she functions.

The exalted human spirit smashes all mental constructs that violate its domain of jurisprudence—the outer senses. All rules against nature or spirit are bound to fail. They lead to neuroses. The girl above had imbibed the sex-repressing lessons and was mentally sure of herself never to succumb to the sexual act, whatever the persuasive capabilities of her lover. Playing the coquette with her lover aroused her sleeping spirit, which inundated both body and mind. All mental constructs—mind stuffing—aimed at checking the natural movements of the spirit were thus smashed. The will of the spirit always prevails. You recall what David said about sex in his lecture above? The girl will naturally propose it, if you flow with events.

My Igbo ancestors knew what I have described above. Natural, sympathetic magic was an open book to them. Compared to them, we are ignoramuses parading as educated and civilized humans. Drunk with the mind-warping doctrines of imported religions, we denigrate and calumniate our wise ancestors. Without studying their sacred science, we call them names—witches, amoosu, amagba, and what not. We are scared stiff because the phenomenon of magic and talismania (amoosu, amagba, ögwü, ökpö) refuses to be wished away by a ranting crowd shouting themselves hoarse with "Holy Ghost Fire!" It looks like the power behind magic is a Holier Ghost Fire.

4
REINCARNATION

WHAT IS REINCARNATION?

Each form is the tabernacle of a spirit to which is attached a self-reflective apparatus or mind. The spirit, being breath, is given a body for action and a mind to embrace the universe in which it dwells. Every form in the universe has a resident spirit and a mind.

A spirit builds typical forms, dwells in those forms, and uses those forms to achieve its principal objective in the general scheme of evolution: to unite mortal with immortal natures. When the human mind merges itself with its associated incarnating spirit (Chi, the Christos), then an anointment and at-one-ment takes place and Christ is born in us. Thus the divine spirit, by this marriage with its associated mind, converts the latter to its own nature. This conversion is the object of the incarnation of spirit in forms. The Ancients symbolized this at-one-ment of the personal spirit and mind by the winged globe: a solar disc (the spirit) with two wings (the bi-polar mind). We mentioned above that sacrifice (Latin: sacra and facio) means "to make sacred", and has no immediate correlation with the denial to oneself of benefits. If privation came in the process of incarnation, it was incidental, not inherent. The spirit legions descended to make a lower order of life holy. Their labor was to sanctify with the gift of divinity the mortal race, and make it immortal and divine.

When a form is worn out, the spirit leaves it and moves on to build a new one. This exit of the spirit is the "death" of the form. Later, this same spirit builds another form in which it dwells, while pursuing its objective. Thus, over time, a spirit incarnates in many forms. A human spirit builds human forms, just as a given tree spirit builds the corresponding tree form. The same is true for all forms—from the speck of dust to suns.

The human form in which a human spirit dwells today may be given a name, say Udoh—a man. This spirit uses that form for, say, 100 years. After 100 years the form is quite old and worn out—Udoh Anaagö is an old man. Effective action through this worn-out form becomes more and more difficult for the spirit and it decides to get out of it, in order to build a new and more vigorous form. In due season, this spirit builds and dwells in a new human form, to which the name Emmanuel is given. Thus the spirit (Chi) which built and dwelt in a human form called Udoh sometime in the past, builds and dwells in a new human form now called Emmanuel.

This movement of a spirit from one form to another is what we call re-incarnation—repeated incarnation of the same spirit over time.

The Ancients understood the process of reincarnation and had a ritual (ï-gba Agü), done by wise ones, for determining the nature and origin of the spirit that has reincarnated in the form of a new human child. We will see in the section on the Agü ritual why the origin of the incarnating spirit is important. The ritual also provided guidelines on what the spirit has come to achieve—the field where the child will excel. The child is not forced to study philosophy when his spirit loves music or some other art. The Christian Bible, in Luke 2:21-32, provides a potent example of this ritual applied to Jesus by the wise one Simeon.

To say that I am the reincarnation of my great-grandfather simply means that the spirit that built and dwelt in the form I label "my great-grandfather" built and dwells in my current form labeled "Emmanuel". A child often inherited the name of some long-dead relative because the same spirit (Chi) that dwelt in the long-dead relative had re-incarnated in the child. A Dibïa Afa once told me: Onye üwa gï bü Chi gï. Shielü onye üwa gï ite na shielü Chi gï ite bü ofu ife. The person whose reincarnation you are is your Chi or God. It is the same thing to cook a meal for your Chi or for the person whose reincarnation you are. My immediate reaction was: But how can a person who died long ago be my Chi or God? The wise Dibïa's words constitute a perfect conundrum until we recall that it is the Chi that moves from one form into another in what we call reincarnation. Chi Emma = Onye üwa Emma, because Onye üwa Emma was the name of the form in which Chi Emma dwelt in Its last incarnation in form.

The ritual for determining which spirit has "come back" generally takes place when the child is one year old. This invaluable ritual has fallen into disrepute because of our so-called civilization, where the healthy practices of our ancestors are desecrated in the name of modern science and pseudo-religion.

Education must be re-visited, because crime is the fruit of a perverted system of education. When crimes occur at home or school, there is need to review our method of education. The child being father to the adult, the adult's mentality is rooted in the child's education. A child unaccepted as he is, can't accept others as they are. Self-acceptance is self-love. He who hates himself can't love others! Healthy education first empowers the mind by developing its capabilities—attention, memory, imagination, thought, will—before stuffing it with concepts and techniques for doing.

What is education? Does the word educate mean:

(a) To empower the mind, by developing its latent capabilities (attention, memory, imagination, thought, will)? or

(b) To stuff the mind with concepts, techniques, tricks and methods of doing?

We all agree that the soil must be prepared before planting anything in it. Without the prior development of the latent capabilities of the mind, the assimilation of concepts and techniques is difficult and destined to fail. But what do we observe in our system of education? We start very early to implant ideas into the unprepared mind of the child. Thus, we stifle the development of the latent capabilities of his mind. It is the lack of this prior preparation of the mind that explains the present dilemma of our system of education—high failure rates, cheating at examinations, recourse to charms, juju, futile prayer sessions, sale of certificates, etc.

Should we not re-think our method of education? In the light of the disappointing results of the current system of education, good common sense advises us to combine the two methods given above, that is:

(1) First, empower the mind, by developing its latent capabilities (attention, memory, imagination, thought, will). This is basic education—the preparation of the soil before planting the

seeds.

(2) Next, teach the mind concepts, techniques, tricks and methods of doing. This is professional education—the actual planting of seeds on the prepared soil.

This approach has the merit of focusing primarily on the maximal development of what is common to all human minds—attention, memory, imagination, thought, will. Prepared in this manner, the youngster will face professional education with a lot of confidence in himself. He will understand, very early, that he is solely responsible for his failure or success. He has a clear idea of what his worth is and comports himself accordingly. He will, thus, no longer have recourse to the usual shortcuts—cheating, powerful success charms, jujus and prayers— which are all snares for the sleepwalker.

Recall that man is made up of a body; a mind, with which he thinks, imagines, decides, etc; and a spirit (Chi), which owns his body and without which he becomes a corpse.

Concerning the spirit, the Bible (KJV) says: "Know ye not that ye are the temple of God, and that the Spirit of God dwelleth in you?" (1Cor. 3:16) "What? know ye not that your body is the temple of the Holy Ghost which is in you, which ye have of God, and ye are not your own?" (1Cor. 6:19) The spirit (Chi) built the body and rules it jealously. Read and meditate Psalm 139, for further insight.

St. Paul tells us, in Romans 7:22, 23 and 25, that the human mind (verse 25) is subject to two laws: (1) The law of God after the inward man or spirit (verse 22); and (2) The law of the body or the law in my members (verse 23).

The mind should learn to understand and not repress sense stimuli. Those stimuli are promptings from the spirit which, like a wind, blows where it wants. Hunger, thirst and sex are prompts from the spirit. To deliberately repress these promptings is to declare war on your own spirit. For the mind to influence the body in any way, it must learn and understand the ways of the spirit who owns that body. Co-operation with the owner of the body—the spirit—is the only way for the mind to have beneficial commerce with that body.

For quite a long time, the civilized world has considered self-control as the key to the eradication of social dis-ease. Physical and mental gymnastics have been devised, with a view to using the will, without the consent of the spirit, to control the body and its senses.

But what degree of self-control has been achieved so far? None! Hypocrisy is the order of the day. Might is right and nations, in spite of international law, engage in armed robbery. Has social dis-ease been eradicated? The reader should judge for himself. Violent crime is rife. The prisons and mental hospitals are packed full of misfits that society has created with its spirit-repressive laws. Is it not time to re-think the social codes that we inherited from our civilized colonial masters, with a view to bringing the left-out human spirit into the picture?

Ten children from one mother are actually created and inhabited by ten different spirits (Chi). The Igbo say: Ofu nne na-amü, mana ö bürö ofu Chi na-eke. Any system of education for these ten children must be flexible enough to take due account of their ten different spirits. Each Chi is unique! A standardized system will always generate misfits and dropouts. The social dis-ease will never be eradicated. The change of approach is worth trying, for the gradual improvement of man and the world he lives in. Let society empower its citizens by helping them bring out what they have within. Education is not mind stuffing to silence the rebellious spirit. Each spirit has something important to contribute in the general construction of the universe, and it takes revenge on society whenever its expression is denied or repressed.

The individual spirit is denied and everybody receives the same training. Mind-stuffing has replaced education. Education comes from "educe" and means to draw out what is within—the spirit. The current mind-stuffing by our systems of education has nothing to do with education since the system takes no account of the individual. The individual spirit, Chi, is so repressed that society is choking with neurotics; hideous crimes abound and punishments for such crimes provide no lasting solutions. The prisons are full of the "criminals" that the society has fabricated and stupid wars rage around the world.

Man has been hypnotized, by vested interest groups, to fight against his own spirit. The result is simply disastrous for all. Well … the spirit is patient and takes its revenge, in due season, on man and his society. We reap what we sow! Provide true education—not mind stuffing—to the children and reap the youth and men who can love themselves and others. Accept people as they are, and they are forced to reciprocate. The old should guide, not rule, the young. The young must live, experiment, make mistakes and learn from their mistakes. The generation communication gap is eliminated by cultivating mutual trust. Trust the child and he will trust you. And when the child trusts, he communicates, asks questions and thus provides the opportunity for the adult to advise him.

When the reality of reincarnation is asserted, Christians protest and say that they have always been taught that man has only one life to live. They were told that after their death, they will go and sit beside God because they went regularly to church, or that they will go to Hell and roast for eternity in the Devil's cooking pot because they did not go to church. If only it was so easy to go and sit at the right hand of God! Why deceive human beings in this manner? In order to console them? But they do not need to be consoled; they simply need to be told the truth.

Belief in reincarnation is basic in ethics or moral law. As long as human beings are not informed about the law of cause and effect which prevails from one existence to the next, all the sermons aimed at changing them for the better will be in vain: they will not change. Whereas if a man knows that the problems and difficulties that come his way in this life are the result of transgressions committed in his previous lives, he will not only accept these difficulties, but he will choose to work for good in order to improve his future incarnations.

REINCARNATION IN THE CHRISTIAN SCRIPTURES

An interpretation of a few passages in the Scriptures will show that Jesus himself knew and accepted reincarnation. You could object and say that you have gone through all the Gospels and that the word "reincarnation" was nowhere to be found. But you will be told that it is not surprising that an explicit mention of the word "reincarnation" was unnecessary at a time when everybody believed in it. How could the Evangelists imagine that they should have spoken specially about reincarnation in anticipation of an epoch when people will no longer believe in it? Their accounts of events are so concise that there was no need to dwell on an issue that was part of the tradition.

Let us consult the Gospels and study some of the questions asked by Jesus or his disciples as well as the answers to these questions.

One day, Jesus asked his disciples: "Whom say the people that I the Son of man am?" [Matthew 17:13-14; Luke 9:18-19]. What does this question mean? Have you ever seen people asking: "Who do people say that I am?" They know who they are and they do not ask themselves what others say about it. To ask such a question, belief in reincarnation must be implied. Now consider the reply of the disciples: "Some say that thou art John the Baptist; some, Elias (or Elijah); and others, Jeremias or one of the prophets". How can one say that a living person is this or that individual who died long ago if the idea of reincarnation is not implied?

At another time, Jesus and his disciples came across a man who was blind from birth, and the disciples asked: "Master, who did sin, this man, or his parents, that he was born blind?" [John 9:2-3]. Here too, how could one ask such absurd questions if one did not believe in reincarnation? When could this man have sinned in his mother's womb? Either the question is just stupid, or it implies the belief in a previous life. Jesus replied: "Neither hath this man sinned, nor his parents, but that the works of God should be made manifest in him". In other words that, passing through this place, I will heal him and the people will believe in me. And he explained to them: You have been taught that men receive punishment for two reasons: either they have sinned and are punished, or else, having committed no sin, they pay for the sins of others, they sacrifice themselves in order to grow spiritually. But there exists a third category of people whose spiritual evolution is complete, they are free and not obliged to come back to earth. But quite often, they come back in order to help humanity. This man born blind belongs to this third category. That is why Jesus said: "Neither hath this man sinned, nor his parents, he came down to earth with this infirmity so that I may heal him and all will believe in me". In this manner, this man born blind would have saved a lot of people.

One day Jesus was informed that John the Baptist was in prison, and the text simply states: "Now when Jesus had heard that John was cast into prison, he departed into Galilee". [Matthew 4:12; Mark 1:14]. Shortly afterwards, John the Baptist was beheaded by Herod. After the transfiguration, the disciples asked Jesus: "Why then say the scribes that Elias (or Elijah) must first come?" And Jesus replied: "Elias truly shall first come, and restore all things. But I say unto you, That Elias is come already, and they knew him not, but have done unto him whatsoever they listed". And the text adds: "Then the disciples understood that he spake unto them of John the Baptist". [Matthew 17:10-13; 11:14]. Thus, it is very clear that John the Baptist was the reincarnation of Elijah. In addition, the Gospels also tell us that when an angel appeared to Zacharias, the father of John the Baptist, to inform him that his wife Elisabeth will give birth to a son, the angel told him: "And he shall go before God in the spirit and power of Elias". [Luke 1:5, 11, 13, 17].

Now let us study the life of Elijah (or Elias), the prophet of fire, in order to find out what he did to merit being beheaded when he reincarnated later in the person of John the Baptist. The story of Elijah and the prophets of Baal is long (I Kings, chapter 18), but here is an extract:

"And Elijah came unto all the people, and said, How long halt ye between two opinions? if the LORD be God, follow him: but if Baal, then follow him. And the people answered him not a word." [I Kings 18: 21] "Then said Elijah unto the people, I, even I only, remain a prophet of the LORD; but Baal's prophets are four hundred and fifty men". [I Kings 18: 22] Having defeated the prophets of Baal in a fire contest [I Kings 18:23-39], the biblical text records that Elijah said unto the people: "Take the prophets of Baal; let not one of them escape. And they took them: and Elijah brought them down to the brook Kishon, and slew them there". [I Kings 18: 40]. Here is the reason why it was to be expected that Elijah will, in his turn, have his throat cut. Because there is a law which Jesus announced in the garden of Gethsemane when Peter drew his sword and cut off the ear of the high priest's servant: "Put up thy sword into the sheath, for all they that take the sword shall perish with the sword". [Matthew 26:51-52; John 18:10; Luke 22:50; Revelation 13:10]. However, the truth in these words is not always recognized during one lifetime. And Elijah, precisely, how did he die? Not only was Elijah not slaughtered by anybody, but a chariot of fire was sent to him and he went up by a whirlwind into heaven. [II Kings: 2:11]. But he received the punishment for his mistake when he came back to earth in the person of John the Baptist. Jesus knew who John was and the fate that awaited him. That is why Jesus did nothing to save him, and did nothing because justice had to follow its course. We now understand why Jesus left the country when he heard that John was thrown into jail: because he was not allowed to save John the Baptist. The law is the law. Each person must carry his cross. [Matthew 10:38].

Jesus said: "Be ye therefore perfect, even as your Father which is in heaven is perfect". [Matthew 5:48]. How could we view this sentence? Either Jesus speaks without thinking by requesting highly imperfect human beings to achieve, within a few years, the perfection of the heavenly Father; or else, he is totally ignorant of who the heavenly Father is and imagines that it is easy to become like Him. In either case, it does not speak well of Jesus. In reality, this sentence also implies reincarnation. Jesus did not think that man was capable of becoming perfect in just one lifetime, but he knew that by constantly wishing for this perfection and working hard to obtain it during many reincarnations, he will eventually attain the goal. The perfection is achieved when man becomes as one of the Gods, i.e., when his mind weds his spirit.

And Moses, what did he write at the beginning of Genesis concerning the creation of man? "And God said: Let us make man in our image, after our likeness; and let them have dominion over the fish of the sea, and over the fowl of the air, and over the cattle... So God created man in his own image, in the image of God created He him." And where is the likeness gone? No doubt, God had the intention to create man in his image and in his likeness, that is perfect as Himself, but he did not do that. He only created man in his image, with the same faculties, but without giving man the plenitude of these faculties or the likeness. Man is in the image of God in that he has wisdom, love and power but these faculties are so small in comparison with the wisdom, love and power of the Creator. But one day, when he develops himself—with time—man will be in the likeness of God and will acquire the plenitude of these faculties. Thus, the passage from the image to the likeness implies reincarnation. God said: "Let us make man in our image, after our likeness", but He did not do so. "God created man in his own image, in the image of God created He him": it is in the absence of the word likeness and the repetition of the word image that Moses hid the idea of reincarnation. [Genesis 1:26-27].

We may gain further insight by going back to what we said about the reincarnating spirit being a "junior God", who later evolves into a "senior God" by the acquisition of a self-reflective mind. At the beginning of its incarnations the "junior God" is made in the image of the "senior Gods": it has a mind like them. When this incarnating "junior God" welds its mind onto itself and is fully self-conscious, it becomes as one of the "senior Gods": it has acquired their likeness. We can now assert that this accomplished "junior God" is made in the image and likeness of the "senior Gods".

Without reincarnation, nothing can be meaningful in religion or in ordinary life. Go to the priests or pastors and ask them: "Please explain to me why one man is rich, handsome, intelligent, strong, why he succeeds in all his ventures, and why another man is sick, ugly, poor, miserable and stupid". They will tell you that it is the will of God. They may also tell you about predestination and grace, but all that explains nothing to you. In any case, it is the will of God. Let us analyze the above reply. Since God gave us some brains, we should not let it rust away.

Thus, the LORD is capricious, He does what He likes. He gives everything to some people and nothing to others. Good, we understand, He is God, it is his will, it is marvelous, we bow. But we fail to understand why later on He is unhappy, furious and outraged when those to whom He gave nothing good make mistakes, become wicked, unbelievers, criminals. Seeing that it is God who gave human beings this mentality, this lack of intelligence or heartlessness, why does He punish them? He who has all the powers, could He not make them good, honest, intelligent, wise, pious, splendid? Not only is it His fault if they commit crimes, but in addition, He punishes them for these crimes! This is where there is something wrong. He has all the powers, He does what He wants, we agree, no one can blame Him for that, but why then is He not more consistent, more logical, more just? He should at least leave human beings alone. Well no, He will throw them into Hell for eternity! And there too, one is stupefied; let us ask ourselves: "For how long did these people sin? Thirty years, forty years? Fine, let them stay in Hell for forty years, not more. But for eternity..., this is incredible cruelty!" We should reason a bit.

Whereas if we accept reincarnation, if we study and understand it, then everything changes. God truly becomes the Master of the universe, the greatest, the most noble, the most just, and we accept that if we are poor, stupid, unhappy, it is totally our fault, because we did not know how to use all that He bestowed on us at the origin, we undertook expensive experiments; and as He, the LORD, is generous and tolerant, He let us get on with it saying: "Well, they will suffer, they will break their heads, but that does not matter, because I will give them again my wealth and my love... they have many reincarnations at their disposal...they are my children and, one day, they will come back." Thus, He let us have our way, and now all the misfortunes that we encounter are of our own making; it is all our fault.

Until the 4th century A.D., Christians believed in reincarnation, just like the Jews, the Egyptians, the Hindus, the Tibetans, etc. But the Church Fathers probably felt that this belief was not quickly producing the expected impact on people, since nobody was visibly in a hurry to improve; and they wanted to push them towards perfection in just one lifetime by suppressing the belief in reincarnation. Moreover, the Church gradually invented horrible things to frighten people, to the extent that in the Middle Ages the only valid belief was in the Devil, in Hell and eternal punishment. Thus, belief in reincarnation was suppressed so as to get people to improve through fear and dread; however, the people did not change, but rather became worse and ignorant above all! It is, therefore, necessary to reintroduce this belief; otherwise, nothing is in focus, nothing jives: life is meaningless, a crazy scheme, and the LORD, who Jesus presented as our Father, appears to be a monster, etc.

The time between two incarnations of the same spirit could be long or short. The Igbo Ögbanje (Ö gba nje), he who returns many times, aptly depicts rapid reincarnation. A child is born today and dies shortly after. The mother gets pregnant again and gives birth to another baby who also dies shortly after. We suspect an Ögbanje is at it again. So, the elders gather and give the dead baby a good cut on its small butt before burial. The mother gets pregnant again and gives birth to a third baby who, o! miracle, has the scar of a good cut on his little butt. And the unmasked ögbanje child will stay, this time around.

The phenomenon of Ögbanje simply shows us that life on Earth and life in a Spirit Guild are analoguous. As we have playmates here on Earth, so do we have playmates there in our Guild. When we incarnate in human bodies we miss our pals back there and they miss us. The link is sometimes so strong that the incarnate spirit exits its body to join its friends back home in the Guild. But the Rulers of the Guild would continue to send the returning spirit back into incarnation until it realizes the futility of trying to avoid the lesson to be learned on Earth. There are other methods, other than cutting some part of the dead baby's body, for handling the Ögbanje phenomenon. Dibïa Ögbanje resolves the issue very rapidly. He identifies the child at birth as Ögbaje and immediate action is taken to avoid the child's inexorable death. The action may consist in unearthing and destroying the Ögbanje pebbles (mpkülü iyi). The child may also receive long razor marks (Nki) on his cheeks, so that his visiting playmates from the Guild would no longer recognize him.

We have noted that spirits are organized in functional hierarchies. Two children from the same hierarchy tend to get on well. The Igbo concept of Ndï Otu (belonging to the same Guild) refers to this functional character of spirits. Otu Ndï Mmili, for instance, refers to the Guild of Water Spirits. The various Igbo Gods (Alüshï) also have their Guilds from which spirits may incarnate in human beings. I had mentioned my granduncle Nweke Alüshï, whose spirit came from the Spirit Guild of Ofufe Amudo, Awka. Spirits from Imöka Awka have incarnated in many Awka children, who pay homage to It before the annual festival. The same is true of Agünaabö Ümüzööcha, Awka. When the spirit of a child comes from an Alüshï Guild, no ancestor shows up during the Agü ritual. This prompts the astute Dibïa to turn to the Alüshï for an answer. A lot is cast (jie ogu) to decide if the reincarnating spirit (Onye Üwa) is ancestral or of the Gods. The search is further narrowed by, determining through the lot, where the God's shrine is located—at the father's or mother's place, Imöka, etc.

It happens also that a living human being could be the Onye Üwa of another person. This is still the Guild phenomenon. The spirit of a living Onye Üwa is simply a very powerful member (say, a Ruler) of the Guild from which the spirit of the baby under investigation has come. Just as Imöka shows up when we interrogate the spirits of many babies, so also would a ruling incarnate spirit show up when we interrogate subaltern spirits from the same hierarchy.

REINCARNATION IN MY FAMILY & THE AGÜ RITUAL

My ancestors understood the process of reincarnation and had a ritual (ï-gba Agü), done by wise ones, for determining the nature and origin of the spirit that has reincarnated in the form of a new human child. But why was it so important to know the nature and origin of the incarnating spirit? The nature of the spirit provided guidelines on what the spirit has come to achieve—the field where the child will excel, his karma, etc. The spirit of a child may come from the father's clan, the mother's clan or some other Spirit Guild. Only spirits from the father's clan can inherit the father's Öfö na Alö and officiate the clan's Ödïnanï rituals. Spirits other than those from the father's clan are strangers to the clan and must go through the ritual of i-go üwa (purchase of onye üwa from the clan) in order to be admitted into the clan. To lead a family, it is not just sufficient for a man to be the eldest son of his father. It is also necessary that his spirit comes from his father's clan. The wisdom of the Agü ritual is evident. No stranger to the clan will head the clan or serve the Gods of the clan, without the appropriate adoption rituals. The Agü ritual tells us who is who in the clan and who can do what for the clan.

I have organized the Agü ritual for all the members of my family. The items required for the inquiry concerning nine persons (three males and six females) were:

(1) The Igbo names of the nine persons, e.g., Kaanaenechukwu Anïzöö
(2) About eight Igbo names (males and females) from the father's side and the mother's side.
(3) Dibïa Afa: two Agü specialists.
(4) Cash: fifty-four Naira (six Naira per person).
(5) Cash: nine 50 kobo coins (4.50 Naira)
(6) Old calabash: broken into nine large pieces. Each piece is

crushed with the heel at the end of the ritual.

(7) Rope: nine pieces.

(8) Ömü (tender yellowish palm frond): one bunch.

(9) Kola nut (four-lobed): nine for the ritual, but there were twenty nuts available.

(10) Yam: eighteen tubers. To the nine tubers used for the ritual proper are added tubers from the remaing nine for the pounded yam to be eaten at the end of the ritual. The unused tubers were given to the Dibïa.

(11) Chicken: three cocks and six hens. Beef to supplement the chickens, ögbönö and requisite soup items.

(12) Gin (njenje): two Congo bottles.

(13) Palmwine (nkwü enu): six gallons (ishibijalï).

(14) Igbo salad: aküofele (leaves of the small version of the garden egg, chopped), ükpaka (finely sliced and slightly fermented oilbean seeds, roasted), azü mkpö (smoked catfish), palmoil, pepper and salt. This salad is consumed before the meal of pounded yam and ögbönö soup.

The Agü process goes like this. The two Dibïa sat on skins placed on the floor and spread out their working tools. The interrogation tool or oracle (mkpükpa) has four elements. Each element consists of a set of four small wooden saucers threaded onto a strong cord. Dried fish vertebrae and metal rings are threaded onto the cord between two saucers. The two Dibïa would simultaneously throw their respective oracles and jointly interpret them. My Ümübeele and Ümüonaga relatives sat facing the Dibïa. My senior brother, Emeke, and I were the only children present. Emeke was called to come forward and "naa Onye Üwa" (take his incarnator). He gave his name as Chukwuemeke Anïzöö and touched the horn (mpu mgbada) held out to him by each Dibïa. Names of men from my clan were examined one after the other, but the two oracles could not agree on any name. We then gave names from Ümüönaga, my mother's village. The two oracles agreed on Özö Ezenwa (Ezeamaalü (na ö ga-echi)), my mother's father, and disagreed on the other names. So, it was decided that Özö Ezenwa is Emeke's Onye Üwa. Or that Emeke is a reincarnation of Özö Ezenwa.

For my absent brother and sisters a man or woman from my clan stood in for them. For my junior brother, Cyril, I touched the horns and gave my name as Uchenna Okwuchukwu Anïzöö. My aunts Ekegboo Nweke (Alüshï) and Nwaamu Nweke (Alüshï) stood in for my six sisters. At the gate of the compound and for each of the nine persons, a piece of the calabsh is crushed with the heel, a branchlet of ömü (the yellow palm frond) is dropped, and the feathers of the cocks and hens are deposited. The complete results are given below:

(1) Rose Chinwe Anïzöba: Her Onye Üwa is Nwaküeri Anïzöba, our grandmother. She was alive when Rose was born. Recall what was written above about this type of reincarnation and about Nwaküeri? She was an indomitable pioneer of the women's liberation movement. She was titled "Eze e-je ögü, ö-chïlï ndï agha ya wünye" (Unable to go to battle, the king/queen sends his/her warriors). Rose is our Nnekwuada (Great Daughter), the rock on which my family rests. Do Rose and Nwaküeri have common characteristics? A lot! But let those who know Rose meditate on the issue, in the light of what we have above on Nwaküeri.

(2) Joy Nneka Anïzöba: Her Onye Üwa is Adaeze Ezelaghö, Nnajide's sister. Sister Joy, Chief Mrs. J.N. Nwokoye (Omelü-öra), is an accomplished retired Civil Servant.

(3) Godfrey Chukwuemeke Anïzöba: Emeke's Onye Üwa is Özö Ezenwa, our maternal grandfather. Brother Emeke is a retired Quantity Surveyor.

(4) Mabel Ögöegbune Anïzöba: Her Onye Üwa is Onyenweenu Umeerie, Anïzöö's mother (my great-grandmother) from Amudo village, Awka. Mrs. Mabel O. Anaje is one of the kindest people I have ever met. She is also an accomplished retired Civil Servant.

(5) Margaret Azüka Anïzöba: Her Onye Üwa is Nwamgboli, wife of Okoye Onyeemeto. Margie is a professor at Unizik Awka, an accomplished intellectual.

(6) Emmanuel Kaanenechukwu Anïzöba: My Onye Üwa is Özö Udo Anaagö Mmadüagwu, my greatgrandfather. He is the Aböshï-udughudu-ngagwu-dï-Igbo-egwu.

(7) Josephine Ifeeyinwa Anïzöba: Ifeyi's Onye Üwa is Onyenweenu Udoh, Anïzöö's sister. Mrs. Ifeyi Okocha is an accomplished retired Civil Servant.

(8) Dorothy Abümchukwu Anïzöba: Dora's Onye Üwa is Anyankwö Nwobu, the lady who brought Agwü Udoh from her mother's home (ikwunne) at Mbaukwu. She was a priest (Ezenwaanyï). Dibïa Afa have asked me why Dora is not Ezenwaanyï. They assert that she will accomplish nothing except she becomes Ezenwaanyï. Agwü Udoh has promised to

help her if she decides to begin implementing her destiny as Ezenwaanyï. She confirmed having the fiber of an Ezenwaanyï, which she was using in some Christian water cult (üka mmili). I hope she would wake up to see that unscrupulous Christian priests are exploiting her natural powers. She is a priest whose God is Anï and whose church and altar are in her own house. Let her note that our Agwü will destroy whatever she builds outside her calling as Ezenwaanyï. Some family members have suggested that she could accomplish the same function as a Christian priest. I replied that she might as well try to wash away the lines on her palms with soap. If she fails to do the Ezenwaanyï in this incarnation, she will have to do it in the next. Ö dï n'öfö! This is the Law, in spite of the say-so of the Christian priest.

(9) Cyril Okwuchukwu Uchenna Anïzöba: Cy's Onye Üwa is Onyeama Ezenwa. He is Özö Ezenwa's most handsome son. He was a playboy, he had blue eyes and died celibate.

The above shows that the spirits of my two brothers, Emeke and Cyril, come from my mother's clan. Emeke and Cyril will remain strangers (they are inlaws!) to the Anaagö clan until their admission into the clan through the "i go üwa" ritual. Folks are surprised to see me breaking the kola nut and pouring libation at the Obi altar, in the presence of Emeke, my senior brother. I simply tell them that ö dï n'öfö, it is in line with the decree of Ndï Ichie. Should I recount the reincarnation and Agü rules given above, just to satisfy the curiosity of a pseudo-Igbo, Igbo n'önü nkïtï? No. A tüölü ömalü, ömalü; a tüölü ofeke, ofekanye ishi n'ofïa. Confronted with a riddle, the initiate understands while the non-initiate divagates into the bush. To avoid unnecessary questions about this situation, I simply present the kola nut tray to him for a blessing touch. And he just says "gaa n'iru" (go ahead).

The following concerns my children.

(1) Rose Nneamaka Ada Anïzöba: Nne's Onye Üwa is Nwaagö Udoh, Anïzöö's sister.

(2) Alexander Chukwuemeke Nwabüishi Anïzöba: Emeke Jr. has Nweke Alüshï as Onye Üwa. Hence both Emeke Jr. and Nweke are incarnations from the Ofufe Amudo Spirit Guild. We have Eucharist feasts with Nweke at the family Obi and pay courtesy visits to the shrine of Ofufe at Amudo village, Awka.

(3) Joy Nkemakonam Anïzöba: Nkem's Onye Üwa is Anyankwö Okoye Onyeemeto. Anyankwö was very gorgeous and was

known as Öchömma. She refused to marry and died celibate.

(4) Robert Chukwukammadu Özöemene Anïzöba: Chuka's Onye
Üwa is my father, Godfrey Nwabüishi Anïzöö.

(5) Moses Obinna Anïzöba: Obinna's Onye Üwa is my grandfather,
Anïzöö Udoh.

We must stop here, since every story has an end. Deeme nu-oo!
Thank you!

5
SATAN OR DEVIL, EKWENSU

Does our theogony exclude Ekwensu, the Devil or Satan? It doesn't, since that God, Satan or Devil, is also a Son of God. Satan as a Son of God belongs to the hierarchy of Ruling Gods.

But what do the Christian Scriptures say about Satan the Tempter (or the Devil)? Let us consult the biblical texts.

Jehovah is synonymous with Satan, as a comparison of II Samuel 24:1 and I Chronicles 21:1 shows. We have:

- II Sam. 24:1 "And again the anger of the Lord was kindled against Israel, and he moved David against them to say, Go, number Israel and Judah."

- I Chron. 21:1 "And Satan stood up against Israel, and provoked David to number Israel."

In the Book of Job, we are told how God authorized Satan to tempt Job's faith; and how Job overcame the temptations and had his blessings doubled. The key chapters and verses are as follows:

❖ Job 1 verse 1: "There was a man in the land of Uz, whose name was Job; and that man was perfect and upright, and one that feared God, and eschewed evil".

❖ Job 1 verse 6: "Now there was a day when the sons of God came to present themselves before the LORD, and Satan came also among them".

❖ Job 1 verse 12: "And the LORD said unto Satan: Behold, all that

Job hath is in thine power; only upon himself put not thy hand."

❖ Job 2 verse 1: "Again there was a day when the sons of God came to present themselves before the LORD, and Satan came also among them to present himself before the LORD".

We are told that Satan destroyed Job's family and property, but Job sinned not nor charged God foolishly.

✓ Job 2 verse 6: "And the LORD said unto Satan: Behold, Job is in thine hand; but save his life."

✓ Job 2 verse 7: "So went Satan forth from the presence of the LORD, and smote Job with sore boils from the sole of his foot unto his crown."

This second time, we are told, Job's faith in God was unshaken in spite of his sufferings. In Job 42, the text relates how God accepted Job and doubled his blessings.

In the Gospels, St. Matthew gives the account of the temptation of Jesus in the wilderness as follows:

Matthew 4 verse 1: "Then was Jesus led up of the Spirit into the wilderness to be tempted of the Devil." [The word Satan is used in Mark 1: 13].

The text gives an account of the three temptations that Satan proposed to Jesus and the answers Jesus gave to the tempter. Having successfully passed Satan's test, the account concludes:

Matthew 4 verse 11: "Then the Devil leaveth him, and, behold, angels came and ministered unto him."

Thus, from the Books of the Christian Bible, we discover that:

(a) Satan is synonymous with Jehovah;
(b) Satan is one of the sons of God, a Benai Elohim;
(c) Satan's job is to tempt;
(d) In spite of Job's holiness, God allowed Satan, His accredited tempter to test Job's faith. Job passed the test and God doubled his blessings;
(e) Before Jesus started his ministry, the Spirit of God brought him before Satan for a test. Jesus passed the test and his ministry began;
(f) Neither Job nor Jesus asked God to spare them from being tempted;
(g) Temptation is crucial in life and particularly in spiritual evolution: it serves to determine what we are capable of.

Satan and his Host constitute the Cosmic Judiciary and Armed Forces. They are the keepers of the Book of Life. The spirits of this hierarchy are responsible for Cosmic Order and the application of incurred Karma. The spirits of vengeance belong to this hierarchy. The Devil or Satan is Ekwensu in Igbo. A smart Igbo philologist gave the following analysis of Ekwensu:

Ekwensu = E kwe n su = E kwe m su = E kwe o su = E kwe ya e-su

Let us consider the key terms in the name:

(1) "E" is the Igbo impersonal subject marker, e.g., E delü = One wrote. E meligo fa = An unspecified subject has defeated them.

(2) "Kwe" is the Igbo verb "to agree", e.g., Kwe na ï ga-eme ya = Agree that you will do it.

(3) "Su" is the verb "to begin suddenly" "to break out", usually a commotion, e.g., Agha e-su = War breaks out.

The name Ekwensu, therefore, means: If one agrees (E kwe), then something breaks out (ya e-su). The Laws are there and they are equally applicable to all. If you decide to break a law, then you have agreed to the commotion that breaks out inexorably. Ignorance of the law does not annul the consequences that accrue from its violation. Ignorance of a law may attenuate, but not annul, the consequences of its violation. One would, for instance, get a sentence of three months of public utility service instead of twelve months behind prison bars.

The God Satan or Devil has a shrine at Anakü (Ekwensu Anakü) in the Ayamelum Local Government Area of Anambra State. Legend has it that folks render themselves invulnerable after a visit to this shrine.

We repeat: Satan and his Host constitute the Cosmic Judiciary and Armed Forces. They are the keepers of the Book of Life. The spirits of this hierarchy are responsible for Cosmic Order and the application of incurred Karma. You may break Nature's Laws and count, as the Christian priest says, on the Blood of Jesus to save you from Satan and his Host. But remember that your Jesus had to pass before this mighty God before he began his ministry. I have heard deluded Christian relatives fighting the Devil or Satan with the Holy Ghost Fire. But the Devil or Satan is exactly the Holy Ghost Fire. So, what a great fight folks!

6
MY PEDIGREE—ONYE MÜ M?

My people ask: Onye mü gï? (Who are your parents?) Our parents are not limited to the father and mother, but extend to the ancestors. I recall presenting myself to an old man as Emma Anïzöba. He asked: which Anïzöba? I said: Anïzöba Udoh. He asked: which Udoh? I replied: Udoh Anaagö. He asked: which Anaagö? I replied: Anaagö Mmadüagwu Ashïï. He smiled and shook my hand three times saying: Ö-ö nne, nna gï mülü gï! (Verily, you are a true son of your father!)

My pedigree is my family tree and describes the line of my ancestors. The Igbo do not generally document their pedigree. Oral data abound and have been the source of unwarranted family feuds. The story varies with each ruling family head. Gradually, the facts are lost in the mists of time. Greedy family members gang up to create fables, with a view to grabbing and selling the property of their brethren. Families have been dispossessed of their birthrights by their unscrupulous relatives. The victims of such robbery usually resort to village heads or the King of the town. The only evidence tendered at these arbitration centers is an oral account of what each party can recall of its ancestry. The verbal testimony of each party is backed by the verbal testimonies of genuine or false witnesses. The marauding party generally hides behind their Christian faith and refuse to swear oaths before the Alüshï.

I had earlier mentioned my grand-uncle's wife, Nwanyanwü Nweke (Özala) from Ümüzööcha village, Awka. This powerful lady helped me trace my pedigree. She personally knew Udoh Anaagö, her father-in-law, and the entire Anaagö Mmadüagwu's descendants. She gave me an elaborate family tree that included women—a rare feat, since only the men count in our genealogy. When the woman marries, her name is lost in the genealogy of her maiden home. Özala was a living encyclopedia and we remained very close until her death. So, what follows is solid stuff.

My traceable ancestral line begins with Maazï Ödïïkpo and his wife Ashïï Nta Nwüwa Öma. Maazï Odïïkpo was a wealthy polygamist whose wives lived in secluded compounds (mkpuke) within the larger walled family compound. Members of the Ümü Ashïï clan of Ümübeele village are the direct descendants of Maazï Ödïïkpo through her wife Ashïï.

The names of the children of polygamists contain two parts: the first part is the name given to the child at birth and the second part is the name of the child's mother. Two boys born to two wives of a polygamist on any Eke market day are named Nweke (Nwa-Eke). To distinguish them the name of the mother is appended to each name. So we may have Nweke be Mgbafö and Nweke be Anyankwö. When the Maazï calls Nweke, he is usually asked: Nweke be onye? (which Nweke?) He then adds: Nweke be Mgbafö, i.e., Nweke of/from Ngbafö. The "be = of, from" is usually omitted and we simply say Nweke Mgbafö, the "be = of, from" is implicit. Ashïï's small compound (mkpuke) is located behind Obi Beele Anwünya (Beelü Önwü) at Enugo Ümübeele. Obi Ümü Ashïï is located in this mkpuke.

Ashïï's eldest son, Mmadüagwu, inherited her mkpuke. Mmadüagwu's eldest son Anaagö, inherited the mkpuke when his father passed on. But Anaagö, a wealthy man too, had four sons and the mkpuke became too small to contain him and his expanding family. He moved out of Ashïï's mkpuke and settled on his vast domain at Egbeana Ümübeele. As mentioned earlier, Anaagö's compound is the last on the Awka-Nibo road before the Öbïbïa River. It is bounded by a deep gully that runs down from Ezi-Udoh square to the Öbïbïa River, the Öbïbïa River itself, and a strip of land that stretches from the cassava ponds (mgboko) before the Awka-Nibo Öbïbïa Ezi-Udoh bridge to Okafö Egbunönü Mgbechi's compound wall, to the end of Ümüökam land that has the same southern limits as Mbgechi's compound. The Ümüökam land comes immediately after Mmadïka Nwözöbïalü Udoh's compound along the road from Ezi-Udoh to the Nibo-Awka road. The following areas are all part of this vast domain:

Mmadïka Nwözöbïalü Udoh's compound and its backyard stretching down to Öbïbïa and containing the giant cotton tree (Akpü Anaagö), the Nwannu spring, the road leading down to Öbïbïa Owele Anaagö; Nwöfö Nwokweghi Udoh's compound and its backyard down to Öbïbïa; Nwammöö Udoh's compound and its backyard down to Öbïbïa, Nnajide Nnabüeze Udoh's compound and its backyard down to Öbïbïa; the central compound occupied by Anïzöö and his brother Nweke (Alüshï) Udoh and its backyard down to Öbïbïa and the bounding gully. This portion includes the land behind the compound of Ejiöfö Okafö (Mma). Across the gully is Mbaanugo's compound and a portion of its backyard stretching towards Öbïbïa Ngene. The latter portion was Anaagö's yam barn, where the echichili trees used for the yam barn pillars are still standing.

Anaagö Mmadüagwu had four sons: Udoh, Ikebüdü, Obudïïke, and Okoye (Onyeemeto). The topography of Anaagö's compound made it partially habitable. The land is on a slope, whose gradient increases as we move towards the Öbïbïa River. Thus, the compound had two portions: a habitable part where houses could be built and a vast non-habitable part stretching to the Öbïbïa River. The non-habitable portion was a virgin forest of palm trees, bamboos, oil-bean trees, breadfruit trees, pear trees, and diverse flora that provided herbal remedies. The threat of uncontrollable erosion made it mandatory to protect this virgin forest standing on the non-habitable portion of the estate. No digging whatever was allowed on the non-habitable area.

Anaagö's eldest son, Udoh, inherited his compound as described above. Ikebüdü moved across the road (dafee ekpe, crossed the ridge) to occupy the following area: Önüzulike's compound and the land immediately behind it towards the Nibo-Awka road, Ibe Chinwuba's compound (where Mbaama Ibe currently lives) and Onwüraa Okechukwu's compound, which was Ikebüdü's residence. Obudïïke moved across the gully to Mbaanugo's compound. Okoye (Onyeemeto) moved out to a land along the road from Ezi-Udoh to Ezi-Nwaafö. This land contains a storey building belonging to this writer. In addition to the above, Udoh inherited Ashïï's mkpuke; Ikebüdü inherited the lands currently occupied at Ümübeele by the Chinwüba family at Ezi-Nwaafö, the Nwezi family, the Akabögü family, and the Eche family.

Ikebüdü had two sons: Önyïdo and Anaagö. This Anaagö Ikebüdü was a reincarnation of his grandfather Anaagö Mmadüagwu. It was customary to give a child the name of the ancestor who reincarnated in the child. We shall call him Anaagö Junior to distinguish him from his grandfather. Ikebüdü's eldest son, Önyïdo, had two sons: Önüzulike and Okechukwu. Anaagö Junior had five sons: Akabögü, Chinwüba, Nwezi, Eche and Udoh. This Udoh was a reincarnation of his grand-uncle Udoh Anaagö and the naming custom was applied naturally. By a rigorous distinction this son of Anaagö Junior would be known as: Udoh (Junior) Anaagö (Junior). Let's put the name simply as Udoh Anaagö Junior, bearing in mind that the epithet, Junior, applies to both the child, Udoh, and his father, Anaagö. Eche and Udoh Junior had the same mother. The sons of Udoh Junior are the only sons of Ikebüdü allowed to partake of Udoh Senior's Agwü Eucharist rituals and feast. Eche, a soft-spoken and kind Dibïa, was a good friend of my father. With only two sons, Önyïdo inherited the following: Önüzulike's compound and the main Ikebüdü's compound now occupied by Onwüraa Okechukwu's family. With five sons, Anaagö Junior inherited the remainder of Ikebüdü's lands comprising the lands currently occupied by: the Chinwüba family at Ezi-Nwaafö, the Nwezi family towards Ashïï's mkpuke, the Akabögü family at Egbeana Ümübeele, the Eche family close to the Ngene Shrine. The land immediately behind Önüzulike's compound and Ibe Chinwüba's compound are all part of Anaagö Junior's inheritance. Udoh Junior later left his elder brother, Eche, and purchased a piece of land facing Ikebüdü's compound at Ezi-Udoh square. Önyïdo's son, Okechukwu, a powerful Dibïa, was now occupying Ikebüdü's compound. His Aröbünaagü's shrine (Ngene Ukwuafö) stood beside the point of entry into the land purchased by his cousin, Udoh Junior. There was, and still is, enough free space on this part of Udoh Junior's land to contain three or more large iron gates. But Okechukwu refused Udoh Junior entry to the land from anywhere along the fence facing his compound, on the grounds that none should disturb his Aröbünaagü's shrine. Thus did Udoh Junior buy a land into which he could not enter, thanks to his cousin's interdiction to use the land's official and sole entry point. The remaining possible entry point was the side of the land facing Ezi-Udoh. But Ezi-Udoh belonged to Udoh Senior, whose son Anïzöö was now in command of the assets of Udoh Senior. Outraged by what Okechukwu did to his cousin, Anïzöö allowed Udoh Junior to enter his land through the Ezi-Udoh square. As a result, the gate into Udoh Junior's compound faces the Ezi-Udoh square. So we now have two Udoh Anaagö's compounds all facing the Ezi-Udoh square. Some of my untutored folks point to Udoh Anaagö Junior as the owner of Ezi-Udoh square. Even the Obi in Udoh Anaagö Senior's compound had been attributed to Udoh Anaagö Junior. The sad part of story of the two Udoh Anaagös is that the eldest of Udoh Junior's surviving sons, Umeadü Udoh-Anaagö, is totally ignorant of his pedigree. His father was the only and original Udoh Anaagö, owner of Ezi-Udoh square! My people say: Ekwe rakalïa önü, e-kwuo oshishi e-ji pïa ya. If the wooden gong gets too loud, we tell it the wood from which it was carved. I had a good opportunity to clarify matters to Umeadü Udoh-Anaagö, in the presence of his clansmen, Ümü Ikebüdü, during a get together in my Obi (the true Obi Udoh Anaagö). Chinwüba Anaagö Junior was a powerful customary chief. He had a prison cell in his Ezi-Nwaafö compound. His sons were Ibe and Ökpala (Nwabe). Ibe's eldest son was Chinwüba, a reincarnation of his father, Chinwüba. His name, Obiesie, was changed to Chinwüba in accordance with the custom. So, we have Chinwüba Junior and his grandfather, the all-powerful Chinwüba Senior. The Junior is Chinwüba Ibe and the Senior is Chinwüba Anaagö Junior. Had the Junior not taken his father's name, Ibe, he would have been called Chinwüba Chinwüba! Legend has it that hired assassins murdered Nwabe, Okpala's mother, along the Awka-Nibo road, on her husband's orders. The woman's arm was smoke-dried and kept as a trophy, which her all-powerful husband displayed publicly. The woman, who sold tobacco (ütaba), got wind of the plot from a repentant member of the group that was detailed to kill her. The hoodlum had asked her for some free snuff expecting her to turn down his request. She gave him as much snuff as he wanted. Moved by her generosity, the hoodlum told her never to go home late because her life was in danger from her husband. Nwabe thanked the hoodlum, closed shop, bought a hen and headed for the famous Raba Shrine at Agülü. She put her life in the hands of Raba, picked up a pebble and went home. Thereafter, she was murdered and her smoked arm was kept as a trophy by her husband. Shortly after, Raba struck in the middle of the night. Raba, the Ezenwaanyï Agülü, led Chinwüba to her waterside where her death-boat was waiting. How art the mighty fallen! His father, Anaagö Junior, was still alive. The next morning wild bees invaded the compound and water rose from the ground. Chinwüba's corpse was abandoned to the bees and rising water. My clansmen met and Dibïa Afa was consulted. They were sent to the Raba Shrine, where the preliminary purification rites were outlined. These initial rites were required to get the bees away, check the water oozing out of the ground, and bury Chinwüba's decomposing body. The legend continues but we shall stop here.

Okoye (Onyeemeto) and his wife Nwamgboli had a son, Emengïnï, and a beautiful daughter, Anyankwö who refused to marry. Nwambgoli's burial rites were financed by Anïzöö, who inherited her husband's assets as per the custom.

Obudïïke had a son, Mbanugo. The latter's sons were: Mmöökwügwö, Chigbata and Chidekwe.

Udoh Anaagö had seven sons: Nwokeke, Nwobu, Nnabüeze, Nwammöö, Nwokweghi, Nwözö and Nwafee. Udoh's eldest son, Nwokeke, died after his marriage and his young childless widow was married (kuchie) by his father, Udoh. From the re-marriage came Anïzöö, his junior brother, Nweke (Alüshï) and their sisters Nwaagö and Onyenweenu. Nweke's mother hails from Amudo village, Awka. An Amudo God (Ofufe Amudo) had reincarnated in Nweke and explains the Alüshï appended to his name. Anïzöö's children were: Nwabüishi (Godfrey), Nwosungene, Ifeöma and Afö-ukwu. Nweke-Alüshï had two daughters: Nwaamu and Ekegboo. Nwobu had a son, Okoye (Mgbolinta) and a daughter, Anyankwö (Mgbolinta). It was Anyankwö who brought Agwü Udoh Anaagö from Mbaukwu, her mother's place (ikwu-nne). Nwobu inherited Ashïï's mkpuke and moved to Enugo Ümübeele. Nnabueze had a son, Nnajide, and a famous daughter, Adaeze Ezelagbö. Nnajide's sons were: Okoye, Obunaabö and Nwa-Ajaana (Jerry). Nwammöö's sons were: Taagbo, Nwajiobu and Ndibe. Nwokweghi's sons were: Nwöfö, Nnenna and Ödükö. Nwözö's sons were Mmadïka and Nnagbo. Nwafee's sons were: Nweke and Ngene.

We have a tradition whereby a non-Awka man may join the clan through the auspices of a rich and powerful member of the clan. It happens like this. I am a wealthy business man based at Achala. An unmarried Achala man works for me and has proved himself worthy to be part of my household. I bring this man to my clansmen and present him as an adopted brother. I perform the requisite adoption rituals and my family name is appended to his name. A non-Awka wife is given to this brother-by-wealth and his residence is somewhere at the backyard of my large compound. He attends the clan's meetings, though he is forbidden to take the floor. He participates in all the family rituals as a special guest. Neither he nor his male descendants can officiate any of the sacred rituals. The adopted brother and his descendants are called Ndï a-kütalü n'ökü (People who came through our wealth). The sacred rule is that whenever it is the turn of my family to head the clan, none of this adopted brother's male descendants will ever lead the clan. To be on the safe side, the adopted brother's male descendant dies or goes blind whenever he becomes a potential candidate to the headship of the clan. I invite my folks to count their teeth with their tongue, to see that the safety mechanism designed to preserve the purity of our traditions has always functioned inexorably. But this practice is never documented and the hard facts soon disappear with the death of those elders who conducted the adoption ritual. With the passage of time the descendants of such adopted brothers start claiming the same leadership rights as the blood-descendants of the clan. Some of these descendants of adopted brothers are loud-mouthed and roguish, thereby betraying their hoodlum ancestry. Agwö, ö ga-amü nwa a-bürö agwö? Waa! Nwa agwö ga-abülïlï agwö! Can the snake's offspring be other than a snake? Never! The snake's offspring will always be a snake! When invited to settle scores by the eternal and inexorable methods of Ödïnanï, these fellows transmute into born-again Christians who would only swear with a Christian Bible. But Ödïnanï is inexorable. Blindness or death awaits the male descendant of an adopted brother who desires to lead the clan. Ö dï n'öfö! The rule is absolute and sacred!

A member of the Ikebüdü family was dismayed when I showed him a copy of my pedigree, at a meeting with them in my Obi. His name is Jimoh Nwoshï Anaagö (Junior). He said his father's name, Nwoshï, and the names of some of his brethren from the Anaagö Junior family were not on the list. These other names were Nwaököödügboo and Nwaokafö Anamakïlïja (Kïlïja). Hum! Were these not Chinwüba Anaagö Junior's hoodlums, Ndï a-kütalü n'ökü? The clan's legend says they are! Jimoh Nwoshi even added that Nwoshï, Nwaököödügboo and Kïlïja were Chinwüba Anaagö's brothers. Chinwüba was the eldest son of Anaagö Junior and his ascertained brothers are: Akabögü, Nwezi, Eche and Udoh Junior. I suggested that the missing names could be Ndï a-kütalü n'ökü (People who came through our wealth). I said that I was not sure, but it was curious that my elders always told me not to delve into such matters, because it was taboo to unveil such family secrets. The subject was e-kumafa, not to be discussed, un-nameable. Fortunately for all of us, key descendants of Chinwüba Anaagö Junior were present at the meeting, viz.: Özö Felix Aneze Chinwüba (Özö Ökpala) and Eng. Pat Nzekwe Ibe. Chinwüba is the grandfather of Özö Ökpala and the great-grandfather of Nzekwe Ibe. I turned to Özö Ökpala who is my age mate and chided him for coming into my Obi with his shoes on. Next, I requested him to help us resolve, now or later, the issue of his granduncles whose names do not appear on my version of our family tree. Özö Ökpala promised to handle the matter and come back to me. He then asked Jimoh Nwoshï to close the matter and relax. I sincerely hope they would clear the muddle, so that our pedigree would get a precious update. Because, the Igbo ask: Onye a-mara ebe mmili bidolu wee-maba ya, kedu ka ö ga-eshi köö akükö nyabü mmili? How can one tell the story of a rain that fell on him, when he is ignorant of where the rain started falling on him?

Another pathetic case was that of Mr. Abole Udeekwe Okoye (Agü) Okechukwu, who was brazenly claiming ownership of the giant cotton tree (Akpü) at Anaagö's backyard near the Nwannu spring, close to the Öbïbïa River. He claims the tree is Apkü Okechukwu, where Okechukwu is his grandfather. I had asked Abole to explain to me and his clansmen how his grandfather, Okechukwu, came to possess a tree at the backyard of the same Okechukwu's great-grandfather? Okechukwu may have claims within the Ikebüdü clan, but he would simply become a common thief by claiming what belongs to other clans within the larger Anaagö Mmadüagwu clan. Abole is a politician and my age mate. I had given him a copy of our pedigree and chided him to go home and find out who he is before approaching vital clan issues with the mythomania that is the bane of our so-called politicians. He refused to remove his slippers in my Obi on the grounds that he is a born-again Christian. Yes, a born-again Christian eyeing his remote pagan ancestor's Akpü tree for sale to timber dealers. A jüghï ajü(jü) wee lie, na-ewete ayaghï aya wee nwüö. He who eats without discernment dies without falling sick.

Below is the report of a spurious committee of some marauding descendants of Anaagö Mmadüagwu, who have been scheming to grab and dispose of the uninhabitable portion of Anaagö's compound. The report is presented "as is". Mr. Aneze Önüzulike, the able secretary of this committee, has the original copy of this report, which the doubting Thomases of my clan should procure. I have provided the details of this part of my family's estate and will not belabor the issue any longer. As indicated above, Anaagö Mmadüagwu settled all his sons by sharing out his landed property among them. The uninhabitable portion of his compound was to remain a virgin forest as already explained. Whoever inherited the habitable portion was Ödïnanï-bound to maintain the physical integrity of both portions of the compound. As the first son (di ökpala) of Anaagö Mmadüagwu, Udoh Anaagö Senior inherited the habitable and uninhabitable portions of this compound. Udoh's brothers, Ikebüdü, Obudïïke, and Okoye Onyeemeto, moved out of their father's compound to their allotted estates as described above. The descendants of Ikebüdü are at fore of this cabal to grab and sell what is not theirs. Except one is a rogue at heart, the claim on Anaagö Mmadüagwu's compound by the descendants of Ikebüdü is simply baffling. Why invent fables to achieve what Ikebüdü himself never attempted in his lifetime? A bunch of pitiable mythomaniacs will always strive to re-tell or re-write history to suit their designs. I have invited all who believe they have a stake in Anaagö's compound to come together for an oath-taking with Öfö and Alüshï. The Ikebüdü family would bring their Öfö and any Alüshï of their choice. I will bring Öfö Udoh Anaagö and any Alüshï of my choice. We shall place the two Öfö and Alüshï together at the village square and then swear to the veracity of our claims. The punishment for false claims would be death and mysery for the false claimants and their families. My proposal turned all the marauding members of the Ikebüdü family into born-again Christians, who would have nothing to do with Öfö or Alüshï. But my Öfö and Alüshï proposal remains the indispensable condition, the sine qua non for the resolution of this cabal to dispossess Anïzöö Udoh Anaagö's inheritors of their birthright. And I hope the somnambulists would wake up to see that they are heading for a stone wall. Kedu ebe e-ji azü e-je? O nweree! Anyï bü nshïkö ji azü e-je ije? Waa! A na-eje ünyaa eje? Waa! Where do you expect to reach by walking backwards? Nowhere! Are we the crab that walks backwards? No! Can we go to yesterday? No!

Before leaving for Europe in 1971 I provided money to my mother for the clearing of the part of the compound occupied by the forest. She was alone on the vast domain and the frightening dwellers of this forest paid her frequent visits. My explanations about our family cult of the forest dwellers did not help much. She was a Christian and a hooded cobra or the African python are dangerous snakes, period. She threatened to move out of the compound if I did nothing about the forest. I authorized her to invite other members of Anaagö Mmadüagwu's family to join her in clearing and farming the land. When I came back in 1980, those descendants of Ikebüdü Anaagö Mmadüagwu that had joined us in clearing and farming the land started laying ownership claims on the land. Under the Chairmanship of Uncle Jerry Ajaana Nnajide, the land was surveyed and plotted for sale to descendants of Anaagö Mmadüagwu. The price of each plot was put at one thousand Naira (N1,000). Uncle Jerry's elder brother, Obunaabö, who was at the head of the Udoh clan, approved the project. He passed on, however, before he could bless (gbaa öfö) the site plan. I had warned Uncle Jerry that his committee is an abomination and there was one punishment for him and his acolytes: Ndï Ichie akpöfugo ügbö unu niine! Your canoes have been perforated by Ndï Ichie. The canoes of the Chairman and seven of his chieftains have sunk already. Ödïnanï is very patient and Its children must learn to be patient. Anï says: tifulu m mkpu, mana rafülü m ögü. Speak out in my defence but leave the fighting for me. I have done my duty and spoken out in defence of Anï.

Erosion is gradually taking over the habitable and non-habitable portions of this estate. My mistake in allowing the clearing and farming of the non-habitable portion dawned on me. The possibility a Nnanka erosion scenario facing us in a very near future frightened me. I called those families who had crops on the land and told them that all farming on the land must cease effective end-December 2005. Ndibe Udoh Junior's wife came to contest my decision saying: Anyï na-akö nyabü ana shite n'igbii. We have been cultivating that land since time immemorial. I drew her attention to the fact that we were in an Obi and then asked her: Kedu mgbe igbii gï bidolu? Ö bükwa ka agha Biafra bulu ka a-nütalü gï? When does your time immemorial begin? Was it not after the Biafra war that we came to marry you? She apologized, took back her words and left. Before end-December 2005, I put Alüshï on the land specifying that:

(1) Farming on the land must cease effective 31 December, 2005.

(2) It is forbidden to appropriate or sell any portion of the land without prior approval from Nwabüishi Anïzöö Udoh Anaagö's family.

Onye kachie ntï, ö fü n'anya! Those who fail to listen, see with their eyes! Onye lie ife abürö nke ya, ö nwüö önwü abürö nke ya! He who eats what is not his, encounters a death that is not intended for him! Mmönwü a-fügo n'ögbö. Onye kwülü a-kwülü, o-mee nye n'arü. Onye gbaa ösö, ö-nüjuo akükö ntï. The masquerade has moved into the arena. You will be whipped if you hang around. Your ears will be filled with news if you run away.

ANAGOR FAMILY LAND: REPORT OF THE COMMITTEE APPOINTED TO CARRY OUT CERTAIN INVESTIGATIONS ABOUT THE LAND AND MAKE RECOMMENDATIONS.

In December 1989, during the Christmas season, members of ANAGOR FAMILY held a meeting. At the meeting allegations were made that pieces or parcels of Anagor Family land, Umubelle village, Awka were being encroached upon and annexed by those whose private compounds adjoin the FAMILY LAND.

Members of the descendants of Anagor Family who own the land are:

(a) Ikebudu Family

(b) Udoh Family

(c) Mbanugo Family (This family has one surviving male alive).

It was Ikebudu and Udoh families that held the meeting in December 1989. At that meeting held in December 1989 members of the family appointed a committee comprising:

i.	JERRY .N. NNAJIDE	(Chairman)
ii.	Aneze Onuzulike	(Secretary)
iii.	Chukwujekwu Nnenna	(Member)
iv.	Onwura Okechukwu	(Member)
v.	Nwanno Okoye	(Member)
vi.	Chidekwe Oduko	(Member)
vii.	Sunday Nwoshi	(Member)
viii.	Obuzoba Akabogu	(Member)
ix.	Chukwukeluo Onuzulike	(Member)
x.	Oguguo Udoh	(Member)
xi.	Christopher Akabogu	(Member)
xii.	Jonathan Onuzulike	(Member)
xiii.	Umeadu Okoye	(Member)
xiv.	Osita Akabogu	(Member)

There were no written Terms of Reference but when the Chairman was briefed about his nomination and appointment as chairman of the committee the purpose was explained to him.

2. During the whole of 1990 the Committee did not meet and could not meet. This was due to the fact that the chairman summoned no meeting: he was seriously looking into his dismissal matter with the Anambra State Government and the eventual Court case over the issue; coupled with his court case in respect or his "Abandoned Property" at Port Harcourt. These two important issues gave him no breathing space.

3. First meeting: First meeting was held on the 5th of May 1991. Members (those that were present) fashioned out the following terms of reference.

(a) To investigate allegations that pieces or parcels of Anagor family land have been encroached upon and annexed into their compound by those whose compounds adjoin the family land. Those suspected of annexing the land are families of Anizoba, Nweke Alushi, Nwanmuo, Onyido and Nnagbo Nwozor.

(b) To investigate the land near Ngene alleged to be annexed by the family of Okoye Mgbolinta.

(c) To investigate the strip of land which the family of Anene Chika claimed.

(d) To investigate and locate the boundary of the entire Anagor family land all round.

(e) To make recommendation as to the use of the entire land.

(f) To consider any other issues relating to the land and make any other recommendation that may assist the family in resolving all issues pertaining to the land.

4. <u>LAND INSPECTION</u>: On the 2nd of June 1991 we commenced inspection of the encroachment and annexations. The first inspected was that claimed by the family of Anene Chika (see item 'C' of the terms of reference). The land involved comprised only two ridges and after inspecting it, the committee handed the parcel to Onwurah Okechukwu and Umeadu Okoye to clear and cultivate it. Onwurah Okechukwu was told by the committee that if he cultivated the land and what he planted was destroyed the committee would refund his expenses.

We also inspected the land near Ngene, claimed and being farmed by the family of Okoye Akutigbueilo. Thereafter the committee inspected the land alleged annexed by the families of Anizoba, Nweke Alushi, Nwanmuo and Onyido. Behind Nweke Alushi the committee saw a property beacon on which was written BI-1155. The beacon is near the wall of Nnajide's compound. The committee took the particulars of the property beacon for investlgation to find out who planted it there.

On the 30th of June 1991 Onwurah Okechukwu and Umeadu Okoye reported that they cleared the bush in the area of the two ridges which late Anene Chika claimed and that later the family of late Anene Chika cultivated part of that area of the two ridges which they cleared. The Committee told them to level the mounds they have made since nothing has been sown or planted therein. On the 8th of September 1991 Umeadu Okoye reported that they planted 'Ogilishi' plants round the area of the two ridges but they were uprooted by unknown person.

The Committee did not pursue this matter further (the area claimed by late Anene Chika family). The Committee left it for the entire Anagor family to take a decision during its general meeting.

<u>ANIZOBA'S COMPOUND</u>:

Beacon BI-1155 was investigated at the survey Division, Ministry of

Works, Lands and Transport Enugu. The Surveyor-General revealed that the private surveyor who owns the initials 'BI' on the beacon was Mr. Nwadiogbu and that he has not filled the survey plan of the land in the Ministry and so the Ministry could not give the Committee a copy of the plan. However it was revealed that the office of Mr. Nwadiogbu was at No. 197 Enugu Road, Awka. Our intension was to obtain the survey plan and know from it who authorised the survey. However on the 22nd of September 1991 we were told by Chukwukeluo Onuzulike (a member of the Committee) who made a private investigation on the beacon that Mrs. Anizoba told him that it was Emma Anizoba who authorised the survey to be carried out on the land. With this revelation the Committee went to Mrs. Anizoba and discussed with her. She confirmed the survey. She told the Committee that when her husband Mr. Anizoba was living, he met the elders: Eche Anagor, Okoye Mgbolinta and others and told them that it was better to bring the grave of ANAGOR into his (ANAGOR's) compound (instead of its remaining outside the compound and kept clean by sweeping every morning). She said the elders agreed and on the day to start the work late Obu Anagor and Mr. Chinwuba Ibe were sent by the elders to supervise the walling in order to make sure that the grave came into the compound. She also confirmed that it was Emma Anizoba who carried out the survey and he (Emma) intended to wall the area from the beacon (BI—1155) linking it to the wall behind their compound which brought ANAGOR's grave into the compound. We asked Mrs. Anizoba to tell Emma not to commence the walling until ANAGOR FAMILY has taken a decision on the matter. She agreed.

As Mr. Chinwuba Ibe was mentioned, the committee took the trouble to see Chinwuba and told him what Mrs. Anizoba said. But Chinwuba denied having gone to supervise the walling at any time. He said, it was not true and that during that time he was not of the age to attend family meeting.

When Emma returned home the committee met him on 20th October 1991 and discussed the issue. He confirmed what his mother told us regarding bringing the grave of Anagor (i.e. Iroko) into his compound. He said it was his father Nwabishi Anizoba who negotiated the whole matter in 1961 when he met the elders who sent late Obu Anagor and Chinwuba Ibe to supervise the walling and to make sure that the grave (i.e. Iroko) came into the compound. He said he was then in secondary II at Okongwu Memorial Grammar School Nnewi. Emma also told the Committee that Chinwuba Ibe saw him on 18th October 1991 to discuss the issue and that when he (Chinwuba) was told everything convincingly he replied that he did not remember whether it was true or not. To drive the matter home Emma suggested to him the taking of OATH (either juju or bible) Chinwuba still replied that he did not remember.

Emma then submitted to us two plans:

(a) Plan No. E.5/AN16/64 made by G.N. Nwokolo surveyor on 22/3/64. This plan is purely a sketch and on examining close, one will see that it shows all the compound of Godfrey Nwabuisi Anizoba in 1964. A copy or this plan is attached as ANNEXEURE A.

It is believed that this sketch plan was made by Godfrey Nwabuisi Anizoba himself before his death.

(b) Plan No. CEN/AN69/90 made by Chidi E. Nwadiogbu, Licensed Surveyor. This is a proper survey plan which on closer examination also shows all the compound of Godfrey Nwabuisi Anizoba in 1990; it supersedes sketch plan No. E.5/AN16/64 [(a) above]. A copy of this plan is attached as ANNEXURE 'B'.

The Committee observed that the shape and boundaries of the compound in plan ANNEXURE 'A' and those in ANNEXURE 'B' are the same and are similar in all respects.

It is the Committee's view that the decision of the elders to bring into the compound the grave of our great great grand father ANAGOR (i.e. the Iroko tree) was a sound one and their decision to send two of their sons to supervise the walling was also sound. It is now left for the general meeting of ANAGOR FAMILY to discuss this matter with a view to issuing instruction, or otherwise, for the completion of the walling by Emma Anizoba.

NWANMUO'S COMPOUND:

It was on the 2nd of June 1991 that we inspected late Nwanmuo's compound. On that day Onwurah Okechukwu and Chukwukeluo Onuzulike, all members of the committee, pointed to the strip of land behind Nnajide's compound which was in fact part of late Nwanmuo's compound. This piece of land measures 36½ft x 75ft, and is bounded by tall Ogilishi trees. This piece of land they said was fenced illegally by Nnajide's family. The Chairman (Mr. Jerry N. Nnajide) who happened to be present at the inspection refuted the allegation and said, it was a blatant lie. He explained the history of that piece of land. He said that the entire Nwanmuo's compound now belongs to him and that he inherited it because he performed the funeral ceremonies (Ikwa-ozu) of late Nwandibe Nwanmuo who was Nwanmuo's most senior son and who died of Leprosy. He said that when Nwanmuo asked for a compound he was given a very narrow piece of land by our great grand elders of ANAGOR FAMILY. He had not developed his compound when late Nwaokweghi was also given land by the elders for his compound. When Nwanmuo saw that Nwaokweghi's land was thrice his own, he complained to the elders that Nwaokweghi's land was thrice his own. The elders inspected the two portions and having discovered the anomaly, gave Nwanmuo the strip behind Nnajide's compound to complement his holding. The chairman said he was told this history by his mother, (late Nwanyangene Nnajide) his aunt (late Nwaudengene Nwanmuo who was Nwanmuo's most senior daughter). The chairman said being a member of the Committee he would like the Committee to refer the matter to his senior brother Obunabor Nnajide who would be in a better position, because of his seniority, to tell the history. The meeting was held in Obunabor Nnajide's house on 22/9/91. Obunabor confirmed that the parcel of land belonged to Nwanmuo but he did not know when the entire compound, including the parcel in question, was given to Nwanmuo. He said that he (Nwanmuo) built his UNO-NGA near Nwaokweghi's UNO-NGA and that a palm tree (still standing, according to him) was near Nwanmuo's UNO-NGA. The meeting pressed and appealed to him to accompany us to the site (Nwanmuo's compound) and show us the particular spot where Nwanmuo's UNO-NGA was built. After much convincing pressure he agreed.

On reaching Nwanmuo's compound Obunabor took us down to the last spot of the compound and showed us where Nwanmuo was buried in the UNO-NGA and it was last inhabited by Nwandibe (Nwanmuo's first son who died of Leprosy).

OBSERVATION: It was observed by the Committee that the UNO-NGA was within the site alleged claimed illegally by Nnajide family and fenced off with Ogilishi not given to him by the elders of ANAGOR FAMILY. Obunabor's statement to the Committee closed the matter. It was not discussed again because there was nothing to discuss.

ONYIDO LAND:

On the 13th of October 1991 the Committee visited late Onyido's land at Odo-ngwo, (Onuzulike family is the descendant of Onyido). Onwurah Okechukwu (a member of the Committee) told the Committee that the land at Odo-ngwo belonged to Onyido and that no other sections or families of ANAGOR FAMILY had gone to that area to cut bamboo tree or tap Ngwo wine. Umeadu Okoye (also a member of the Committee) supported Nwaonwurah Okechukwu by saying that right from his boyhood he knew that that land belongs (and still belongs) to Onyido family. This parcel of land extends from bamboo tree down stream in that area to Akpu tree further upland. There was further evidence by Chukwukeluo Onuzulike that the Ngwo trees in that area were being tapped by one Nwokeonyema and Ude both of Nibo for Onyido.

OBSERVATION:

The Committee observed that the land from the evidence before it, does not belong to ANAGOR FAMILY.

OKOYE MGBOLINTA'S LAND:

This land which is near Ngene juju was the next discussed. This land was alleged to be ANAGOR FAMILY land but claimed and annexed by Okoye Mgbolinta whose family still farms the land. Umeadu Okoye and Nwanno Okoye (members of the Committee) sons of Okoye Mgbolinta told Committee that their father got the land from Umuike people by PLEDGE i.e. Umuike land owners pledged the land to their father for money. They went further to say that their mother, before she died, had warned them that if Umuike placed juju on the land they should not remove but if they (Umeadu and Nwanno) placed juju on the land and if the juju was removed by Umuike people, they (Umuike people) should take the land. The land is known as Mgbamgba-Uba.

Onwurah Okechukwu had a different view. He said that the land belonged to ANAGOR and that when ANAGOR shared his land among his family none went to Okoye Mgbolinta and that he was told to take that land and that since then the land was still with him. Again, Umeadu Okoye and Nwanno Okoye said if we were in doubt we could ask Mgboli Ezenagu. We went to Mgboli on the 20th of October 1991. She confirmed that Mgbamgba-Uba land belonged to Okoye Mgbolinta but that she did not know how he got the land and that Okoye's wife had been cultivating the land.

OBSERVATION:

We closed this matter after visiting Mgboli and hearing from her as we could not proceed to investigate it further. Because, according to Onwurah Okechukwu, if it is true that ANAGOR asked Okoye Mgbolinta to take the land after sharing his other lands and none went to Okoye, then it belongs to Okoye. It should therefore not be queried by anybody.

NNAGBO NWOZOR'S COMPOUND:

On the 17th of November 1991 we investigated the portion of Anagor's land alleged occupied by Nnagbo family. We asked him John

(Nnagbo's son) the boundary of the land. He said he did not know. But members, who knew, showed him the portion of Anagor's land which they appropriated into their compound. As the mother was not in we could not proceed but we took the measurement of the land which is 11ft x 101ft.

When we went back to Nnagbo's compound on 22/12/91 we met John's mother, showed her the original end of Nnagbo's compound and also the portion of Anagor's land she encroached and appropriated into the compound. She denied encroaching upon and appropriating any land. Instead of driving home her denial conclusively and convincingly she resorted to accusing Onwurah that he did not know the boundary of Nnagbo's land because he (Onwurah) was all the time living at Nibo and only came back recently.

OBSERVATION:

The Committee felt that Mrs. Nnagbo's excuses and denials were flimsy. There was physical existence of where the boundary wall terminated and where the encroachment took off. The Anagor general meeting should make a clear decision on this after visiting the land.

RECMMENDATIONS:

1. We recommend that ANAGOR FAMILY should summon a general meeting at which this report should be read and deliberated upon. The meeting should take meaningful decisions on the observations of the Committee arising from its various investigations of land suspected annexed into compounds of Anizoba/Nweke Alushi, Nwanmuo, Onyido, Nnagbo and Okoye Ngbolinta.

2. The Committee was of the opinion that the general family meeting of Anagor Family should look into the entitlement to the land of Mbanugo family. The Committee felt that the bone of contention which made the land to remain undivided all these years was because some sections of Anagor family claimed that the land should be divided into two, one for Ikebudu and the other for Udoh, while others claimed that it should be divided into three portions: One for Ikebudu, another for Udoh and the third for Mbanugo. Because the elders could not agree on the method of division made the land to remain undivided till this time.

3. The Committee recommended that the entire lend should be made into a layout of plots by the Anagor family. The family should take a decision in this respect. They should also lay conditions

for allocating/selling the plots to each of Anagor's family descendants who have no family residential plot and who desire to have an abode in Awka.

The land is bounded as follows:

(a) Eastern boundary: Umu-uzegbo family and Umuokam family lands.

(b) Southern boundary: Obibia Stream

(c) Western boundary: Umuokam family land further down the Obibia stream and Egbunonu's family land further up land.

Signed:

i.	JERRY .N. NNAJIDE	(Chairman)	(Signature)
ii.	ANEZE ONUZULIKE	(Secretary)	(Signature)
iii.	CHUKWUJEKWU NNENNA NWOKWEGHI		
		(Member)	(Signature)
iv.	ONWURAH OKECHUKWU	(Member)	(Thumbprint)
v.	NWANNO OKOYE	(Member)	(Signature)
vi.	CHIDEKWE ODUKO	(Member)	(No Signature)
vii.	SUNDAY NWOSHI	(Member)	(Signature)
viii.	OBUZOBA AKABOGU	(Member)	(No Signature)
ix.	CHUKWUKELUO ONUZULIKE	(Member)	(Signature)
x.	OGUGUO UDOH	(Member)	(No Signature)
xi.	CHRISTOPHER AKABOGU	(Member)	(No Signature)
xii.	JONATHAN ONUZULIKE	(Member)	(Signature)
xiii.	UMEADU OKOYE	(Member)	(Signature)
xiv.	OSITA AKABOGU	(Member)	(Signature)

7
CARE OF THE BODY AND THE MIND

CARE OF THE BODY

It is essential to cultivate a healthy body and mind. Externally, the body and the clothes we put on it must be clean. Internally, the bowels and other elimination systems must function properly, with a view to ensuring the optimal evacuation of wastes. To drink a cup of water on waking in the morning will enhance health and protect us from tricky stomach problems. Brown rice, black-eyed beans cooked with palm oil, some bran, a fruit or piece of raw cabbage taken before food enhances the digestive potentials of the stomach. We will rarely strain at stool.

We should solemnly feed the body. Chatting or watching the television while feeding the body simply shows we have no regard for it and its owner—the spirit. Our attention should rest on the action at hand, i.e., feeding the body. This one thing I do —I am feeding my body!

Eat whatever is available in your geographical location. Whatever firewood you have will cook your meal. Tow the middle path in diet. Avoid the extremes of starving or stuffing the body.

The object of physical exercise is to adjust the spine and further oxygenate the body. A long silent walk will suffice, if one cannot afford to jog or do something vigorous. If a walk is not feasible, then try this for the health of the spine—the source and cure of dis-ease:

(1) Lie on your stomach, on the bed or floor, with a pillow placed under your chest. Place the jaw at the edge of the pillow, making sure that the mouth and nose are unobstructed by the pillow. Place both palms one on top of the other just above the forehead. Let the upper and lower teeth come together naturally, to help support the weight of the head. Let the tongue touch the palate. Put both legs together, with thighs, knees, heels and big toes touching each other. The toes and top of the feet should be as flat as possible on the bed or floor. This is the initial position.

(2) Tense the muscles of both legs by squeezing the butt and bending the feet downward at the ankles, as if to touch some object with the tip of the toes. This tenses the muscles of the waist, thighs, calf and feet. Do this muscle tensing about five times. You will feel a pull along the spine from the back of the head to the feet. Relax, but don't change the initial position of the body.

(3) With both legs still touching each other, and without lifting the trunk, gently fold the legs backward at the knees, as if to touch the lower back with the heels. Do this gently for a number of times. Fold back each leg in turn in the same way. Again relax, but keep the initial position.

(4) Raise the head and chest on your elbows, with the abdomen/genitals flat on the bed and legs touching each other. Observe the pull on the spine from the neck to the lower back. With legs touching each other, gently fold them backward at the knees. Do this gently for a number of times. Gently swing the joined, folded legs sideways and note the pull at the waist. Fold back each leg in turn. Lower the head and chest on the pillow; assume the initial position and relax.

(5) Fold the arms and cross the palms on the pillow. Place the jaw on top of the crossed palms. Hold the teeth together and let your crossed palms bear the full weight of your head. Gently roll the head sideways, using the jaw as a pivot. This helps to release blocked neck vertebrae with a pleasant rap. Look up and roll your eyes to relax the nerves that go into and out of the brain through the first cervical vertebra—the atlas. Notice the pull at the back of the head and neck. With legs touching each other, gently fold them backward at the knees. Do this gently

for a number of times. Fold back each leg in turn in the same way. Stay in this position—with the arms and palms crossed on the pillow and the jaw placed on top of the crossed palms—for about five minutes. Uncross your palms and assume the initial posture, face down, legs touching, with your jaw on the edge of the pillow, mouth and nose unobstructed. Relax. If you fall asleep, then enjoy it. You will wake up a new person!

The above exercise should not take more than thirty minutes, excluding the refreshing sleep time at the end of step (5). We may also lie on the stomach for at least thirty minutes daily, or as often as possible (while reading or watching television) to prevent the spine from becoming bent to one side or the other. The spine as the source and cure of dis-ease is presented in the section on Healing in Appendix C of the author's book: The Second Birth. The Mind Is A Bag. How Loaded Is Yours? by Trafford Publishing.

The Tongue

We have probably been accustomed to think of the tongue as the organ of taste, or for moving food around in the mouth, or as an organ of speech. Here is another use of the tongue which is almost magical in its results in making the body magnetic.

When not in use in speaking or eating the tip of the tongue should be in contact with the roof of the mouth.

Why? Placing the tip of the tongue against the roof of the mouth is like closing an electric switch. As a result, the nerve fluid from the solar plexus flows over the nerves that extend from it to the tongue; and from the tongue these vibrations are carried to the brain over the nerves which come directly from the brain to the roof of the mouth. This love vibration relaxes the cells of the brain, awakens them to renewed activity and causes them to draw in more energy from the universe, and to radiate it over the nerves to all parts of the body. Thus, the body is made more magnetic, and increased resistance to heat and cold is assured.

When the tip of the tongue is in contact with the roof of the mouth, the opening from the nose to the lungs is made larger, and the upper lobes of the lungs are more completely filled by air than when the tongue is permitted to lie flat in the mouth.

This practice is beneficial during meditation as it ensures a good flow of nerve fluid between the head and the rest of the body. It is also of very great value to singers and speakers, because it brings the thyroid muscles into greater activity, and makes them stronger.

CARE OF THE MIND

The states of the mind

The outer senses are ruled by the spirit, while the mind is mandated to educate the inner senses with the help of the spirit at its disposal—the attention. This is why the mind has difficulty affecting the outer senses directly with the will. It is only through its spirit component that the mind can impact the body and its senses. The mind need not bother to educate the outer senses, since they belong to the spirit and the latter knows how best they should be.

But ignorance has deluded man to believe that the outer senses can be controlled by conscious effort of will. The mind has thus been engaged in a futile battle against an omnipotent spirit. The result of the battle is the acquisition of the ego, dis-ease in mind and body, social unrest and misery.

The brain is the organ of the mind. The states of consciousness or mind are associated with electrical activity in the brain. This electrical activity is displayed in the form of brainwaves, measured by an electroencephalograph (EEG). The rhythms of this energy are measured in cycles per second (CPS).

The states of mind are waking, relaxed, and sleeping. To these states of mind are associated certain categories of brainwaves. Generally, brainwaves of 15 CPS and above are called Beta waves; nine to fourteen are Alpha; five to eight Theta; and four and below are Delta.

When we are wide awake, doing and achieving in the workday world, we are in Beta, or outer consciousness. When we are daydreaming or just going to sleep but not quite there yet, or just awakening but not yet awake, we are in Alpha, or inner consciousness. When we are asleep we are in Alpha, Theta, or Delta. With some training we can enter the Alpha level at will and still remain fully alert. This is a key step in mind training.

We may note that the above states of the mind can be simply described as depicting the volatility—rate of change—of the mind's attention. In Beta or waking consciousness, the mind is fully alert and the volatility of its attention is maximal. This volatility decreases as we enter the Alpha, Theta and Delta levels of consciousness. For further insight, see author's book: The Second Birth. The Mind Is A Bag. How Loaded Is Yours? Trafford Publishing.

Silence

In the individual efforts to study the world within, silence has always been regarded as an aid. It is a true saying that speech is silver, silence is golden, for more can sometimes pass in silence than in speech, however eloquent. Too much, indeed! That is why lovers are afraid of their silences, and why in tense moments people are driven to take refuge in meaningless talk and laughter; their silence would reveal too much. Society owes its existence more to the fear of solitude than to the love of sociability; people assemble because they cannot endure the thought of being left alone with nothing to do. Television, radio, reading, solitaire—these are a few of the devices employed to postpone the inevitable and fateful moment when one must be alone with himself.

If at that moment of aloneness one has the courage to raise the last drawbridge, to interrupt all external communications, and become isolated in his own inmost fortress to re-become at last the Silent Watcher (the Spirit or Witness) that no barrier can keep long at bay, he will unknowingly have taken the first step on the spiritual path.

Silence and stillness of attention have the effect of conserving all the bodily forces usually wasted in unnecessary speech and action. We become for the first time conscious of the rhythmic flow of life's forces, and are able to hear the faint music they make on the harp of the body, inaudible before because of our own noisiness and restlessness. We become aware of having entered a condition of peace wherein our passions lose their power, and the worm in the brain ceases to squirm. It is this conservation of energy carried on over a long period, which gives the true Adept his look of coiled power, of youthfulness, however old in years he may be. But more is involved than the storing up of energy ordinarily uselessly expended. There is the presence of a more subtle and powerful force: psychic energy or spiritual ardor, which can produce phenomena.

Counting backward steadies attention

Lie comfortably on your back. Gently close your eyes. Ensure the tongue is in contact with the palate. Slowly, at about two-second intervals, count backward from one hundred to one. As you do this, keep your attention on it. If you lose the trail, go back to the last number you can recall as having been counted and continue from there. If you are not sure, just start again from one hundred. Do this for fifteen minutes, twice a day—upon waking in the morning and before sleeping at night.

You may fall asleep during the exercise. That simply shows how tired you are. Enjoy the sleep. Continue the exercise later. Set your alarm for fifteen minutes later in case you drift off to sleep during the morning exercise. With practice sleep will no longer intrude and the attention can be focused solely on the counting.

Ideas that have nothing to do with counting may pop up in the mind asking for attention. Gently ignore them and use the will to keep the attention uniquely on counting. It's tough, but this is basic. Nothing can be achieved without polarizing the attention.

Use the hundred to one method for one week. Then count only from fifty to one, twenty-five to one, then ten to one, and finally five to one, one week each. Move to the next method only when you have completely mastered the previous one. The fifty to one method should be done only when the hundred to one is completely mastered.

Note that when the exercise is mastered we are able to move from the Beta level of consciousness to the Alpha level by simply counting from five to one. The counting helps us to get a handle on the volatility of the mind's attention. A quick entry into the Alpha or relaxed state of mind is all we need for mental creativity.

Listening steadies attention

Sit quietly and just listen to the sounds around. Put your attention into just listening.

For the morning session, sit silently and gently close your eyes. Ensure the tongue is touching the palate. Now experience quietly all that is happening around and do nothing else. You are hearing sounds?—listen to them silently. A bird is singing—listen to it silently; the breath is moving in and out—go on watching it silently: nothing else has to be done

The night session has to be done while lying down in bed. The steps are exactly those of the morning session, i.e., listening, being a witness. Lying silently on your bed, gently close your eyes. Close your lips and ensure the tongue is in contact with the palate. Now experience quietly all that is happening around and do nothing else.

You will hear the cry of a bird, you will hear the loud music from your neighbor's apartment, the barking of a dog, and many other sounds—just keep listening silently. It is just as if there is an empty room and a sound comes in, resonates and goes. You should not think about why you are hearing these sounds; neither should you think about why the dog is barking, because you have nothing to do with the dog. There is no reason for you to think about why this dog is barking or why this stupid dog is disturbing you now that you are meditating. No, you have nothing to do with it. The dog does not know at all that you are meditating: he has no idea about it, he is absolutely innocent, he is just doing his job. It is nothing to do with you. He is just barking, so you have to let him bark. It is not a disturbance to you unless you make it a disturbance. It becomes a disturbance only when you resist, when you want the dog to stop barking—the trouble begins there. The dog is barking, it should bark. You are meditating, you should meditate. There is no conflict between these two, there is no opposition. You are silent and the dog's sound will come, linger, and go; it is not a disturbance to you. Just accept that the dog is barking and listen silently. Drop the resistance. Accept its barking. And the moment you accept it, the barking of the dog is transformed into a musical rhythm.

So do not resist. Listen silently to whatsoever is all around This silent listening is a very miraculous phenomenon. This non-resistance, this non-opposition towards life is the clue to the polarization of attention.

Give attention to only one thing: "I am listening. I am listening totally to whatever is happening. I am not doing anything else, just listening, totally listening."

Listening is stressed because as you listen totally, the attention is placed exclusively in the sense of hearing. I am listening, and this one thing I do. So put your total effort into listening. This is a positive effort.

During the listening exercise, some sense other than hearing may solicit the mind's attention. Ideas may just pop up from memory. If you try to throw out the ideas then the mistake which we just spoke about will start happening. It is a negative effort. Ideas cannot be thrown out by making an effort to get rid of them, but if they are simply noticed and given a passing attention, they will fade away. While listening, the mind must give maximum attention to stimuli coming from the sense of hearing; stimuli from other senses are noticed and ignored.

Then do only one thing: listen silently to whatever sounds are coming from all around. A bird will make a sound, a child will speak on the road—listen to them silently. Go on listening and listening and listening, and everything will become silent inside. Listen—listen silently for ten minutes. Let all the attention be on listening. Be just listening, doing nothing else.

Here's a recapitulation of the night session: First of all lie down with your body totally relaxed. Allow it to be completely loose and relaxed. Then slowly close your eyes. Ensure that the tongue is in contact with the palate. Now for ten minutes remain awake inside and keep listening silently to all the sounds around. Stay awake inside, don't go to sleep. Remain conscious inside. Stay awake inside and keep listening silently. Just keep listening. Keep listening to the silence of the night and while listening, a deep emptiness will arise. Drown in the emptiness that is all around until the mind has become completely empty.

Note that even while listening to someone else you may be full of your own thoughts. That is "false hearing." Then you are not a listener. You are only under the illusion that you are listening, but as a matter of fact you are not.

For "right hearing" it is necessary for the mind to be in a completely silent state of watchfulness. The mind's attention must be stilled. When you are only listening and not doing anything else, only then are you able to hear and understand. If it does not happen in this way, you are not listening to anyone but yourself—you remain surrounded by the tumult raging within you. And when you are engaged in such a way nothing can be communicated to you. Then you appear to be seeing but you are not; you appear to be listening but you are not.

Christ has said, "Those who have eyes to see, see. Those who have ears to hear, hear." Did those he was talking to not have eyes and ears? Of course they had eyes and ears, but the mere presence of eyes and ears is not enough for seeing and for hearing. Something more is needed and without it the existence or non-existence of eyes and ears is the same. That something more is inner silence and attention. It is only when these qualities are there that the doors of the mind are open and something can be said and heard.

Once you have learned this kind of hearing, it becomes your life-long companion. It alone can rid you of trivial preoccupations. You can awaken to the great mysterious universe outside and you can experience the eternal, infinite light of awareness hidden behind the tumult of the mind.

Right seeing and right hearing are the foundation of all right living. Just as everything is clearly reflected in a lake that is totally calm, without ripples, that which is the truth, that which is the divine will be reflected in you when your mind becomes calm and still like the lake. And the mind becomes calm when its volatile attention is fixed or polarized.

The mind is the kingdom of heaven spoken of in the Christian Bible and the training of the mind's attention is achieved by the use of the force of the will.

We find in Matthew (11:12): "And from the days of John the Baptist until now the kingdom of heaven suffereth violence, and the violent take it by force."

We also find the location of this kingdom of heaven in Luke (17: 20-21):

20. Now when He was asked by the Pharisees when the kingdom of God would come, He answered them and said, "The kingdom of God does not come with observation;

21. nor will they say, 'See here!' or 'See there!' For indeed, the kingdom of God is within you.

In the spiritual school headed John the Baptist (John the Baptizer) the kingdom of heaven suffereth violence, because the students had to use the violence of the will to overcome the volatility of the mind's attention. By forcing his attention to be still, man takes his mind (his kingdom of heaven) by force.

THE FATEFUL MONTHS OF THE YEAR

The months of March, June, September, and December seem to have something fatal about them. Crazy things just happen in these months. Could there be something special about these months that has eluded our consideration?

Recall the assassination of the Roman Emperor Julius Caesar in 44 BCE. Caesar summoned the Senate to meet in the Theatre of Pompey on the Ides of March, i.e., 15th day of March. A certain seer warned Caesar to be on his guard against a great peril on that day, saying: "Beware of the Ides of March!" When the day came and Caesar was on his way to the senate-house, he greeted the seer with a jest and said: "The Ides of March has come," and the seer said to him softly: "Yes, the Ides of March has come, but it has not past." As the Senate convened, Caesar was attacked and stabbed to death by a group of senators who called themselves the Liberatores (Liberators); they justified their action on the grounds that they committed tyrannicide, not murder, and were preserving the Republic from Caesar's alleged monarchical ambitions.

Recall the Tenerife air disaster of March 27, 1977, when two Boeing 747 airliners (KLM and Pan Am) collided at Los Rodeos on the island of Tenerife, Canary Islands, Spain, killing 583 people. The accident has the highest number of fatalities (excluding ground fatalities) of any single accident in aviation history. We are told that the KLM attempted takeoff, even though the Pan Am was still on the runway and the KLM had not received clearance for takeoff. The Pan Am tried to get out of the way and the KLM tried to climb over, but the latter ended belly up after dragging its tail on the ground. The lower fuselage of the KLM plane hit the upper fuselage of the Pan Am plane, ripping apart the center of the Pan Am jet nearly directly above the wing. This accident seems crazy, and it is!

Recall also:

(1)   The June 23, 1985 Irish Sea destruction of an Air India plane en route to Bombay that killed 329 people;

(2)   The December 21, 1988 Lockerbie, Scotland destruction of a Pan Am flight killing 270 people;

(3)   The June 23, 1993 annulment of President M.K.O. Abiola's election by General I.B. Babangida and the ensuing political turmoil that engulfed Nigeria;

(4)   The December 22, 1999 destruction of Odi in Nigeria's Niger Delta region;

(5)   The December 23, 1999 military coup in Côte d'Ivoire;

(6)   The September 11, 2001 destruction of the twin towers of the World Trade Center in New York City, USA;

(7)   The September 19, 2002 eruption of armed rebellion in Côte d'Ivoire;

(8)   The March 19, 2003 invasion of Iraq by Great Britain and the USA;

(9)   The December 26, 2004 Indian Ocean undersea earthquake that triggered a series of devastating tsunamis along the coasts of most landmasses bordering the Indian Ocean, killing 229,866 people in eleven countries, and inundating coastal communities with waves up to 30 meters (100 feet) high. It was one of the deadliest natural disasters in history.

The above are instances, but the curious reader may consult a time-line of world history for further insight.

We repeat: The months of March, June, September, and December seem to have something fatal about them. Crazy things just happen in these months. Could there be something special about these months, which has eluded our consideration? My answer is: Yes, there is something special about these months, which has eluded our consideration. They are the Fateful months for our planet Earth and its inhabitants.

And Fate is inexorable!

I, therefore, invite all to be careful during the following four periods of the year: the two solstices (June and December) and the two equinoxes (March and September). Why? Just have a good look at the orbit of the Earth around the Sun. This orbit is an ellipse with two axes, like a rugby ball. The two solstices are situated at the ends of the major axis of the ellipse, while the two equinoxes are placed at the ends of the minor axis. In its yearly travel around the Sun the Earth has to negotiate four bends represented by the equinoxes and the solstices.

Look well again at the rugby ball and you may understand the dangers that confront our planet every year at those bends. The Earth's speed round the Sun is about 30 kilometers per second. But this speed is not uniform along the ellipsoid orbit. Just as a motor vehicle reduces its speed to negotiate a deep corner, the same is true for the Earth. The corners at the solstices of June and December are so deep and sharp that the Earth comes to a quasi-standstill in order to go safely through them. It is this quasi-standstill of the Earth that gives us the impression that the Sun is standing still. Hence the name of Solstice (sol = sun, sistere = come to a stop) given to this period of the year. It is this extreme application of its brakes that upsets the magnetic fields on the Earth's surface. The same is true at the corners of the equinoxes but the magnitude of the magnetic disturbance is less, compared with that of the solstices.

Everything on Earth is upset during these four periods, because the survival of the planet is at stake and its Guiding Spirit Host (Anï) is having a hard time; just like the articulated truck driver struggling mentally and physically to steer his vehicle through a deep road bend. Great disasters occur during these four periods of the year. Crazy things "just" happen during these four periods. Coup and terror plotters operate during these periods.

The feasts of Christmas (December), Easter (March), St. John the Baptist (June) and St. Michael (September) were instated to remind Christians of the need for retreat and meditation at the approach of these fateful periods. Unfortunately, our business-minded spiritual guides have taught us to engage in all sorts of excesses during these periods. These feasts relate to the four cardinal points on the Earth's orbit and are older than any religion. The Sages of old instituted them for the benefit of mankind. Certain laws are at work on Earth during the four periods and these laws affect us inexorably as inhabitants of the planet, whatever our religion may be.

The focal dates are: 21 March, 21 June, 21 September and 21 December.

My advice: keep sacred the ten days before and after these fateful dates. Leave your home only when it is absolutely necessary. Meditation, Moderation, Retreat and Silence are advised. The Gods help only those who help themselves! Had I known is the brother of Mr. Late! Orimili na-eli onye ö-fülü ükwü ya! The sea swallows those whose feet it sees!

8
CONCLUSION

I believe we have reviewed what is required to understand Ödïnaï, in spite of unsuccessful attempts by our Christian guests to destroy our very roots. We have given a clear and robust conception of Deity, the universe and man, which is the rock on which Ödïnanï rests. We also saw the efforts being made in my Awka home to revive Ödïnanï. There is still plenty of mental house-cleaning to be done, but the message is taking hold. Anï is a God and, like all Gods, Its ways are not the ways of men.

The role of Dibïa Afa in Ödïnanï is primordial. People complain that majority of them are liars and cheats. Maybe! But one sage told me: Dibïa niine na-ashï ashï, mana ï fü Dibïa nya shïalü gï ashï maka na üfödü ashï na-abü ezi okwu. The Dibïa are liars, but when you come across a Dibïa tell him to lie for you, because some lies are true. The Dibïa is a trained seer, just like a trained Tarot card reader. The Tarot cards have fixed meanings. The position of each card in a spread also has a fixed meaning. The only variable element is the sequence in which the consultant picks the cards from the Tarot pack. Assume we are using only the twenty-two major trumps to interrogate the invisible. I shuffle the twenty-two cards and place them facing down on a table. I then ask you to pick four cards, one at a time, and give them to me without looking at the image on the card. I place the cards on another table in the form of a cross, the cross spread. The second card faces the first across the short arm of the cross, while the third and fourth cards are placed opposite each other at the top and foot, respectively, of the long arm of the cross. A fifth card, which is a summary of the four cards, is placed in the center of the cross. When you went to pick the cards, something moved your hand to blindly pick a card among twenty-two cards. The same something moved your hand when you blindly picked the three other cards. But the something that was blindly moving your hand is simply your Chi or God within your body. Your Chi knows the answers to your queries. It uses the cards that you choose and the sequence in which you choose them to answer the relevant query. The Tarot reader simply reads out what your Chi is showing through the cards. The same is true of the Dibïa Afa.

Remember that the Dibïa Afa does not have all the answers. We listen to the Dibïa without surrendering our reason. Ask questions, if you don't understand what the Dibïa is saying. Onye ajüjü a-nara efu üzö. He who asks questions never misses his way. The implementation of his recommendations must be dependent on our sole judgement. That's why my folks say: a gbachaa afa, a chïköö uche. Deliberation must follow the afa session. A minimum of three different Dibïa Afa should be consulted for important issues. A comparison of the three oracles would give a good indication of what to do.

I repeat: God in manifestation is, like the Army, a Host of fashioning Powers or Gods. Prayer to a God yields immediate results, while prayer to God yields nothing.

My name is Anï zöba m. Anï is my savior. I know that Anï is an unfailing God. He who is with a God fears nothing. I call on all Igbo to repent and return to their roots in Ödïnanï. It is their only road to salvation.

Ibe anyï-ee! Ibe anyï ekenee m unu-oo! I greet all Igbo people!

APPENDIX

A SAMPLE ÖDÏNANÏ RITUAL

Standardized songs and prayers for the worship of God and saints is an absurd Judeo-Christian contraption that has no place in Ödïnanï. In Ödïnanï, Chukwu is the boss and container of the various functional Chi (which include Anï and Alüsï). The Alüsï, being functional Chi, perform specific functions – procreation, protection from mishap, provision of wealth, health, justice, retribution, etc. The prayers and songs offered to these functional Gods are function-specific. A war-prayer or war-song is offered to a war-God.

The dictionary tells us that the word "worship" means treating somebody or something as divine and showing respect by engaging in acts of prayer and devotion. But this definition of the term "worship" has no place in Igbo theosophy, because the Igbo functional Gods are not worshiped at all. Instead of worship, the Igbo enter into pacts with their functional Gods. If the God does "this" for me, then I will do "that" for the God.

For instance, a woman who wants a son would enter into a pact with the God of procreation. She will promise to celebrate the God periodically with the required consumables (cash, food, drinks, etc.), if she conceives and safely delivers a male child within, say, the next one year. She also asks the God to take back Its gift (the male child) if she breaks her promise to come and celebrate after safe delivery. This pact process is called ï-gö-mmöö (to negotiate with, navigate – not worship – the functional Gods or Spirits).

Akwalï Ömümü is my clan's God of fertility and childbirth. When a man from my clan gets a wife, he takes her to the God's shrine and asks the God for male and female children and for their safe delivery. Remember that there were no maternities and the birth of children happened at the backyard under the care of our astute Granny-midwives. A child may die at birth, but the mother must remain alive to bear other children.

This God is celebrated once every year by the clan. All our wives come with cooking utensils. A man whose wife has given birth to two boys and a girl will bring three four-lobed kola nuts, alligator pepper, palm wine, gin, firewood, two cocks, one hen, three smoked catfish, and three yams. If you have ten children, each male child presents a cock and each female child presents a hen. Each child brings a tuber of yam, a smoked catfish and one four-lobed kola nut. The alligator pepper, firewood, palm wine and gin have no strict rules for the quantities that may be provided, since we are celebrating. Each mother sets up her fireplace around the shrine where she will prepare her favorite soup – egusi, öra, ögbönö, nsala, etc. Some people bring rams and goats too.

With the kolanut-bowl in his hands, the priest (officiating elder) sits before the holy earth-mound symbolizing the God and gives thanks for our children and their trouble-free delivery. He implores the God to continue to give us children and protect our women from death during childbirth; the newly-married couples now come around the mound to present gifts (kola nuts or gin) to the God. To check-out whether the God agrees with what is going on, the priest breaks a four-lobed kola nut and throws the lobes into the kolanut-bowl. The spread of the lobes is an oracle that shows acceptance or rejection of the ceremony by the God. With the acceptance of the God ensured, the priest proceeds to slaughter the animals. The blood is sprinkled over the mound and the clan's öfö, while the carcasses are taken away by young men for cleaning, cutting-up and sharing-out to the women for the preparation of soups. The priest pours palm wine and gin libations on the mound and outside the shrine (for uninvited spirits), and the drinks are then served to the public. The amalü-ile (efficacy) prayer is offered and involves the sharing of smoked catfish soaked in salted peppery palm oil. The yams are cooked and pounded in readiness for the Eucharist feast. The pounded yam and soups are presented in front of the earth-mound and the priest asks the God to flow into the food for the Eucharist feast to continue. The priest takes some food (pounded yam, soup, and meat) in the altar plate, tastes the food and loudly affirms that it is delicious. He then places four small pieces of meat, gizzard and liver on the earth-mound. The same number of pounded yam lumps are soaked in the soup and placed on the mound. One soup-soaked lump of pounded yam and a piece of meat are thrown outside the shrine for uninvited spirits to share. The food is then shared out to everybody present, including non-clan members. There is so much to eat and drink that the women bring food-flasks and jerry-cans to take food and palm wine back home. At the close of the feast the clan breaks into a hilarious dance as the priest intones an appropriate song, as follows:

Akwalï anyï akwalï anyï-oo
Iyolo-oloo
Akwalï anyï-oo
Iyolo-oloo
Anyï ga-elie
Iyolo-oloo
Arö özö-oo
Iyolo-oloo
Anyï ga-elie
Iyolo-oloo
Anyï a-müö n'udo-oo
Iyolo-oloo
Anyï ga-elie
Iyolo-oloo
Anyï a-müö nwoke-oo
Iyolo-oloo
Anyï ga-elie
Iyolo-oloo
Anyï a-müö nwaanyï-oo
Iyolo-oloo
Anyï ga-elie
Iyolo-oloo

Akwalï anyï-oo
Iyolo-oloo
Anyï ga-elie
Iyolo-oloo

Dear Reader, do you want the above song in English? Okay, but are you not asking me to give you a wife/husband and the mat on which both of you will sleep? Let's share the burden. I will provide the key elements and you fill the gaps.

Akwalï anyï = Our Akwalï
Anyï ga-elie (ga-eli ya) = We shall celebrate it
Iyolo-oloo = an onomatopoeia describing the effortless gliding out of the baby during delivery (chïrïrïï-wereree)
Arö özö-oo = Next year-oo
Anyï a-müö n'udo-oo = If we deliver children safely
Anyï a-müö nwoke-oo = If we deliver males
Anyï a-müö nwaanyï-oo = If we deliver females

Can you see how the song fits the occasion? We are negotiating with the Akwalï Ömümü and we shall celebrate it if our requests – safe delivery of males and females – are fulfilled.

Daalü nü. Thank you.

ISBN 1425176611-9

9 781425 176112

Made in the USA
Middletown, DE
13 June 2017